AF177791

Tales of
Crime and Mystery

Cornelsen

Tales of Crime and Mystery

Autor
Dr. Paul Maloney, Hildesheim

Redaktion
Katrin Gütermann

Umschlaggestaltung
orangerie-grafikdesign

Layout und technische Umsetzung
Annika Preyhs für Buchgestaltung+, Berlin

www.cornelsen.de

Diese Werk berücksichtigt die Regeln der reformierten Rechtschreibung und Zeichensetzung. Ausnahmen bilden Originaltexte, bei denen lizenzrechtliche Gründe einer Änderung entgegenstehen.

Die Webseiten Dritter, deren Internetadressen in diesem Lehrwerk angegeben sind, wurden vor Drucklegung sorgfältig geprüft. Der Verlag übernimmt keine Gewähr für die Aktualität und den Inhalt dieser Seiten oder solcher, die mit ihnen verlinkt sind.

1. Auflage, 2. Druck 2016

Alle Drucke dieser Auflage sind inhaltlich unverändert und können im Unterricht nebeneinander verwendet werden.

Druck: H. Heenemann, Berlin

ISBN 978-3-06-0335238-8

CONTENTS

Abbreviations and Symbols

AE	American English	**l., ll.**	line, lines
BE	British English	**n**	noun
adj	adjective	**p., pp.**	page, pages
derog	derogative	**pl**	plural
e.g.	(Latin) exempli gratia = for example	**sb.**	somebody
fml	formal	**sl**	slang
infml	informal	**sth.**	something
jdn., jdm.	jemanden, jemandem	**v**	verb
		Webcode	can be entered at www.cornelsen.de/webcodes to connect you directly to a specific download

Dear student,

In the collection at hand you will be taken on a tour of one of the most popular genres of modern fiction: stories of crime and mystery.

In the first story, 'A Scandal in Bohemia' by Arthur Conan Doyle, the world-famous 'consulting detective' Sherlock Holmes engages in a battle of wits with an unusual opponent: a beautiful woman. After reading the story, you will compare it with the television adaptation from the popular series 'Sherlock', in which Doyle's plot is translated from Victorian England to the fast-moving world of international terrorism and digital technology.

In the second story in the collection, 'The Tell-Tale Heart' by Edgar Allan Poe, the narrator takes you by the hand as he plans and carries out a brutal murder. Poe's classic tale of a 'perfect crime' that comes back to haunt the criminal has lost nothing of its morbid fascination.

H. H. Munro's 'The Open Window', in which a timid visitor has the bad luck to be left alone with a teenage girl who possesses an unusual talent, is not only one of the shortest, but also one of the best ghost stories ever written. The text is presented as an audio recording. While listening, close your eyes and try to imagine yourself in the foggy twilight of an evening in autumn, when strange things can occur.

The final story of the collection, Daphne du Maurier's thriller 'The Birds', takes you to the wind-swept plains of post-war Cornwall, where one man and his family fight a desperate battle against an unexpected enemy. In spite of its age, du Maurier's story addresses questions about civilization and nature that strike us today as surprisingly modern. The author's skill at creating suspense and an atmosphere of danger won her the attention of Alfred Hitchcock, whose film of the same name is based on du Maurier's story.

While you are dealing with the texts in this collection, you will be given the opportunity to practise core skills that you need for your final exam: summary writing, analysis of narrative perspective and characterization, listening comprehension and mediation.

The author also hopes that you will enjoy the stories presented here and that at least once you will feel a pleasurable chill running down your spine.

1 A Scandal in Bohemia

ARTHUR CONAN DOYLE

In the following story, a mysterious client asks
'consulting detective' Sherlock Holmes to solve a seemingly
unsolvable problem.

I

To Sherlock Holmes she is always *the* woman. I have seldom heard him
5   mention her under any other name. In his eyes she eclipses and predomi-
nates the whole of her sex. It was not that he felt any emotion akin to love
for Irene Adler. All emotions, and that one particularly, were abhorrent to
his cold, precise but admirably balanced mind. He was, I take it, the most
perfect reasoning and observing machine that the world has seen, but as a
10   lover he would have placed himself in a false position. He never spoke of the
softer passions, save with a gibe and a sneer. They were admirable things for
the observer—excellent for drawing the veil from men's motives and actions.
But for the trained reasoner to admit such intrusions into his own delicate
and finely adjusted temperament was to introduce a distracting factor
15   which might throw a doubt upon all his mental results. Grit in a sensitive
instrument, or a crack in one of his own high-power lenses, would not be
more disturbing than a strong emotion in a nature such as his. And yet there
was but one woman to him, and that woman was the late Irene Adler, of
dubious and questionable memory.
20   I had seen little of Holmes lately. My marriage had drifted us away from
each other. My own complete happiness, and the home-centred interests
which rise up around the man who first finds himself master of his own
establishment, were sufficient to absorb all my attention, while Holmes,
who loathed every form of society with his whole Bohemian soul, remained
25   in our lodgings in Baker Street, buried among his old books, and alternating
from week to week between cocaine and ambition, the drowsiness of the
drug, and the fierce energy of his own keen nature. He was still, as ever,
deeply attracted by the study of crime, and occupied his immense faculties
and extraordinary powers of observation in following out those clews, and
30   clearing up those mysteries which had been abandoned as hopeless by the
official police. From time to time I heard some vague account of his doings:
of his summons to Odessa in the case of the Trepoff murder, of his clearing
up of the singular tragedy of the Atkinson brothers at Trincomalee, and
finally of the mission which he had accomplished so delicately and success-
35   fully for the reigning family of Holland. Beyond these signs of his activity,
however, which I merely shared with all the readers of the daily press, I knew
little of my former friend and companion.
     One night—it was on the twentieth of March, 1888—I was returning
from a journey to a patient (for I had now returned to civil practice), when

---

title *Bohemia:* Königreich
Böhmen

5 *eclipse sth./sb.:* make sth./
sb. appear insignificant

5 *predominate:* have the
highest status

6 *akin to sth.:* related to sth.

7 *abhorrent:* verhasst

11 *gibe* [dʒaɪb]: unkind
remark

11 *sneer (n):* unpleasant look
that expresses disrespect

12 *veil* [veɪl]: Schleier

13 *intrusion:* Störung,
ungebetenes Eindringen

15 *grit:* dirt, very fine sand

18 *the late Irene Adler:*
implies that Adler is no
longer alive at the time of
writing. However, it could
also mean that her name is
no longer Irene Adler, as she
is now married.

19 *memory:* (here) reputation

24 *loathe sth.* [ləʊð]: hate sth.
very much

24 *Bohemian:*
unconventional

26 *drowsiness:* state of feeling
sleepy

27 *fierce:* intense

28 *faculty:* power, ability

29 *clew* = clue

32 *summons:* official
document calling for sb. to
appear in person

33 *Trincomalee:* city in Sri
Lanka

35 *reign (v)* [reɪn]: herrschen

my way led me through Baker Street. As I passed the well-remembered door, which must always be associated in my mind with my wooing, and with the dark incidents of the Study in Scarlet, I was seized with a keen desire to see Holmes again, and to know how he was employing his extraordinary powers.

5 His rooms were brilliantly lit, and, even as I looked up, I saw his tall, spare figure pass twice in a dark silhouette against the blind. He was pacing the room swiftly, eagerly, with his head sunk upon his chest and his hands clasped behind him. To me, who knew his every mood and habit, his attitude and manner told their own story. He was at work again. He had risen

10 out of his drug-created dreams and was hot upon the scent of some new problem. I rang the bell and was shown up to the chamber which had formerly been in part my own.

His manner was not effusive. It seldom was; but he was glad, I think, to see me. With hardly a word spoken, but with a kindly eye, he waved me to an

15 armchair, threw across his case of cigars, and indicated a spirit case and a gasogene in the corner. Then he stood before the fire and looked me over in his singular introspective fashion.

"Wedlock suits you," he remarked. "I think, Watson, that you have put on seven and a half pounds since I saw you."

20 "Seven!" I answered.

"Indeed, I should have thought a little more. Just a trifle more, I fancy, Watson. And in practice again, I observe. You did not tell me that you intended to go into harness."

"Then, how do you know?"

25 "I see it, I deduce it. How do I know that you have been getting yourself very wet lately, and that you have a most clumsy and careless servant girl?"

"My dear Holmes," said I, "this is too much. You would certainly have been burned, had you lived a few centuries ago. It is true that I had a country walk on Thursday and came home in a dreadful mess, but as I have changed

30 my clothes I can't imagine how you deduce it. As to Mary Jane, she is incorrigible, and my wife has given her notice, but there, again, I fail to see how you work it out."

He chuckled to himself and rubbed his long, nervous hands together.

"It is simplicity itself," said he; "my eyes tell me that on the inside of your

35 left shoe, just where the firelight strikes it, the leather is scored by six almost parallel cuts. Obviously they have been caused by someone who has very carelessly scraped round the edges of the sole in order to remove crusted mud from it. Hence, you see, my double deduction that you had been out in vile weather, and that you had a particularly malignant boot-slitting spec-

40 imen of the London slavey. As to your practice, if a gentleman walks into my rooms smelling of iodoform, with a black mark of nitrate of silver upon his right forefinger, and a bulge on the right side of his top-hat to show where he has secreted his stethoscope, I must be dull, indeed, if I do not pronounce him to be an active member of the medical profession."

45 I could not help laughing at the ease with which he explained his process of deduction. "When I hear you give your reasons," I remarked, "the thing always appears to me to be so ridiculously simple that I could easily do it

2 *wooing (old-fashioned):* time when a man courts a woman he wants to marry

3 *A Study in Scarlet:* the first novel featuring Sherlock Holmes

5 *spare:* schlank, hager

6 *blind (n):* Jalousie

7 *swift:* quick

7 *eager:* excited

13 *effusive:* overly friendly

15 *spirit case:* small cupboard containing alcoholic beverages

16 *gasogene:* apparatus for making soda water from tap water

17 *introspective:* looking inward, lost in thought

18 *wedlock:* marriage

18 *suit sb.:* be right/good for sb.

21 *fancy sth.:* imagine sth., believe sth.

25 *deduce sth. (from sth.):* etwas (aus Indizien o.ä.) schließen

31 *give sb. notice:* jdm. kündigen

35 *score sth.:* etwas ritzen

39 *malignant:* bösartig

39 *specimen:* Exemplar

40 *slavey:* girl servant who does the lowest tasks

41 *iodoform:* organic substance with a strong smell, formerly used as a disinfectant

41 *nitrate of silver:* inorganic substance formerly used as an antibiotic

42 *bulge:* Wölbung

myself, though at each successive instance of your reasoning I am baffled until you explain your process. And yet I believe that my eyes are as good as yours."

"Quite so," he answered, lighting a cigarette, and throwing himself down into an armchair. "You see, but you do not observe. The distinction is clear. For example, you have frequently seen the steps which lead up from the hall to this room."

"Frequently."

"How often?"

"Well, some hundreds of times."

"Then how many are there?"

"How many? I don't know."

"Quite so! You have not observed. And yet you have seen. That is just my point. Now, I know that there are seventeen steps, because I have both seen and observed. By-the-way, since you are interested in these little problems, and since you are good enough to chronicle one or two of my trifling experiences, you may be interested in this." He threw over a sheet of thick, pink-tinted note-paper which had been lying open upon the table. ' It came by the last post," said he. "Read it aloud."

The note was undated, and without either signature or address.

"There will call upon you to-night, at a quarter to eight o'clock," it said, "a gentleman who desires to consult you upon a matter of the very deepest moment. Your recent services to one of the royal houses of Europe have shown that you are one who may safely be trusted with matters which are of an importance which can hardly be exaggerated. This account of you we have from all quarters received. Be in your chamber then at that hour, and do not take it amiss if your visitor wear a mask."

"This is indeed a mystery," I remarked. "What do you imagine that it means?"

"I have no data yet. It is a capital mistake to theorize before one has data. Insensibly one begins to twist facts to suit theories, instead of theories to suit facts. But the note itself. What do you deduce from it?"

I carefully examined the writing, and the paper upon which it was written.

"The man who wrote it was presumably well to do," I remarked, endeavouring to imitate my companion's processes. "Such paper could not be bought under half a crown a packet. It is peculiarly strong and stiff."

"Peculiar—that is the very word," said Holmes. "It is not an English paper at all. Hold it up to the light."

I did so, and saw a large "E" with a small "g," a "P," and a large "G" with a small "t" woven into the texture of the paper.

"What do you make of that?" asked Holmes.

"The name of the maker, no doubt; or his monogram, rather."

"Not at all. The 'G' with the small 't' stands for 'Gesellschaft,' which is the German for 'Company'. It is a customary contraction like our 'Co'. 'P', of course, stands for 'Papier'. Now for the 'Eg'. Let us glance at our Continental Gazetteer." He took down a heavy brown volume from his shelves. "Eglow,

1 *baffled:* completely confused

16 *chronicle sth.:* record sth. in writing

17 *pink-tinted:* rosa gefärbt

23 *moment:* (here) importance

26 *quarters:* sources

27 *take sth. amiss:* be upset/ angry about sth.

31 *insensibly:* without noticing it

35 *well to do:* rich

37 *half a crown:* old British coin

37 *peculiar:* eigentümlich

Eglonitz—here we are, Egria. It is in a German-speaking country—in Bohemia, not far from Carlsbad. 'Remarkable as being the scene of the death of Wallenstein, and for its numerous glass-factories and paper-mills.' Ha, ha, my boy, what do you make of that?" His eyes sparkled, and he sent up
5 a great blue triumphant cloud from his cigarette.

"The paper was made in Bohemia," I said.

"Precisely. And the man who wrote the note is a German. Do you note the peculiar construction of the sentence—'This account of you we have from all quarters received.' A Frenchman or Russian could not have written
10 that. It is the German who is so uncourteous to his verbs. It only remains, therefore, to discover what is wanted by this German who writes upon Bohemian paper and prefers wearing a mask to showing his face. And here he comes, if I am not mistaken, to resolve all our doubts."

As he spoke there was the sharp sound of horses' hoofs and grating
15 wheels against the curb, followed by a sharp pull at the bell. Holmes whistled.

"A pair, by the sound," said he. "Yes," he continued, glancing out of the window. "A nice little brougham and a pair of beauties. A hundred and fifty guineas apiece. There's money in this case, Watson, if there is nothing else."
20 "I think that I had better go, Holmes."

"Not a bit, Doctor. Stay where you are. I am lost without my Boswell. And this promises to be interesting. It would be a pity to miss it."

"But your client—"

"Never mind him. I may want your help, and so may he. Here he comes.
25 Sit down in that armchair, Doctor, and give us your best attention."

A slow and heavy step, which had been heard upon the stairs and in the passage, paused immediately outside the door. Then there was a loud and authoritative tap.

"Come in!" said Holmes.
30 A man entered who could hardly have been less than six feet six inches in height, with the chest and limbs of a Hercules. His dress was rich with a richness which would, in England, be looked upon as akin to bad taste. Heavy bands of astrakhan were slashed across the sleeves and fronts of his double-breasted coat, while the deep blue cloak which was thrown over his
35 shoulders was lined with flame-colored silk and secured at the neck with a brooch which consisted of a single flaming beryl. Boots which extended halfway up his calves, and which were trimmed at the tops with rich brown fur, completed the impression of barbaric opulence which was suggested by his whole appearance. He carried a broad-brimmed hat in his hand, while
40 he wore across the upper part of his face, extending down past the cheek-bones, a black vizard mask, which he had apparently adjusted that very moment, for his hand was still raised to it as he entered. From the lower part of the face he appeared to be a man of strong character, with a thick, hanging lip, and a long, straight chin suggestive of resolution pushed to the length of
45 obstinacy.

1 *Egria:* Doyle's name for the town of Eger in Bohemia

3 *Wallenstein = Albrecht Wenzel von Wallenstein (1583–1634):* Bohemian general during the Thirty Years' War; protagonist of Friedrich v. Schiller's Wallenstein trilogy

10 *uncourteous:* impolite

18 *brougham* [ˈbruːəm]: type of carriage

18 *beauties:* beautiful horses

19 *guinea* [ˈgɪni]: old British gold coin

21 *Boswell:* allusion to James Boswell (1740–1795) who wrote a biography of his friend Samuel Johnson

33 *astrakhan:* fleece of a karakul lamb

34 *double-breasted:* zweireihig

34 *cloak:* Umhang

35 *silk:* Seide

36 *brooch:* Brosche

36 *beryl:* semi-precious stone used in jewellery

37 *calf (pl. calves):* lower part of the leg

39 *broad-brimmed hat:* Hut mit breiter Krempe

41 *vizard mask:* mask that covers the upper part of the face

44 *suggestive of resolution pushed to the length of obstinacy:* giving him the appearance of someone whose strong will made him stubborn

"You had my note?" he asked with a deep harsh voice and a strongly marked German accent. "I told you that I would call." He looked from one to the other of us, as if uncertain which to address.

"Pray take a seat," said Holmes. "This is my friend and colleague, Dr. Watson, who is occasionally good enough to help me in my cases. Whom have I the honor to address?"

"You may address me as the Count Von Kramm, a Bohemian nobleman. I understand that this gentleman, your friend, is a man of honor and discretion, whom I may trust with a matter of the most extreme importance. If not, I should much prefer to communicate with you alone."

I rose to go, but Holmes caught me by the wrist and pushed me back into my chair. "It is both, or none," said he. "You may say before this gentleman anything which you may say to me."

The Count shrugged his broad shoulders. "Then I must begin," said he, "by binding you both to absolute secrecy for two years; at the end of that time the matter will be of no importance. At present it is not too much to say that it is of such weight it may have an influence upon European history."

"I promise," said Holmes.

"And I."

"You will excuse this mask," continued our strange visitor. "The august person who employs me wishes his agent to be unknown to you, and I may confess at once that the title by which I have just called myself is not exactly my own."

"I was aware of it," said Holmes drily.

"The circumstances are of great delicacy, and every precaution has to be taken to quench what might grow to be an immense scandal and seriously compromise one of the reigning families of Europe. To speak plainly, the matter implicates the great House of Ormstein, hereditary kings of Bohemia."

"I was also aware of that," murmured Holmes, settling himself down in his armchair and closing his eyes.

Our visitor glanced with some apparent surprise at the languid, lounging figure of the man who had been no doubt depicted to him as the most incisive reasoner and most energetic agent in Europe. Holmes slowly reopened his eyes and looked impatiently at his gigantic client.

"If your Majesty would condescend to state your case," he remarked, "I should be better able to advise you."

The man sprang from his chair and paced up and down the room in uncontrollable agitation. Then, with a gesture of desperation, he tore the mask from his face and hurled it upon the ground. "You are right," he cried; "I am the King. Why should I attempt to conceal it?"

"Why, indeed?" murmured Holmes. "Your Majesty had not spoken before I was aware that I was addressing Wilhelm Gottsreich Sigismond von Ormstein, Grand Duke of Cassel-Felstein, and hereditary King of Bohemia."

"But you can understand," said our strange visitor, sitting down once more and passing his hand over his high white forehead, "you can understand that I am not accustomed to doing such business in my own person. Yet the matter was so delicate that I could not confide it to an agent without

---

4 *pray (old-fashioned):* please

11 *wrist:* Handgelenk

20 *august* [ɔːˈɡʌst] (adj, fml): hochstehend

25 *of great delicacy:* sehr heikel

26 *quench sth.:* stop sth. before it can spread

27 *compromise sb.:* embarrass sb.

28 *implicate sb.:* involve sb.

28 *hereditary* [həˈredɪtri]: ererbt

31 *languid:* very relaxed

32 *incisive:* clear-thinking

35 *condescend:* sich herablassen

38 *agitation:* nervous excitement

47 *confide sth. to sb.:* jdm. etwas anvertrauen

putting myself in his power. I have come *incognito* from Prague for the purpose of consulting you."

"Then, pray consult," said Holmes, shutting his eyes once more.

"The facts are briefly these: Some five years ago, during a lengthy visit to
5 Warsaw, I made the acquaintance of the well-known adventuress, Irene Adler. The name is no doubt familiar to you."

"Kindly look her up in my index, Doctor," murmured Holmes without opening his eyes. For many years he had adopted a system of docketing all paragraphs concerning men and things, so that it was difficult to name a
10 subject or a person on which he could not at once furnish information. In this case I found her biography sandwiched in between that of a Hebrew rabbi and that of a staff-commander who had written a monograph upon the deep-sea fishes.

"Let me see!" said Holmes. "Hum! Born in New Jersey in the year 1858.
15 Contralto—hum! La Scala, hum! Prima donna Imperial Opera of Warsaw— yes! Retired from operatic stage—ha! Living in London—quite so! Your Majesty, as I understand, became entangled with this young person, wrote her some compromising letters, and is now desirous of getting those letters back."

20 "Precisely so. But how—"

"Was there a secret marriage?"

"None."

"No legal papers or certificates?"

"None."

25 "Then I fail to follow your Majesty. If this young person should produce her letters for blackmailing or other purposes, how is she to prove their authenticity?"

"There is the writing."

"Pooh, pooh! Forgery."

30 "My private note-paper."

"Stolen."

"My own seal."

"Imitated."

"My photograph."

35 "Bought."

"We were both in the photograph."

"Oh, dear! That is very bad! Your Majesty has indeed committed an indiscretion."

"I was mad—insane."

40 "You have compromised yourself seriously."

"I was only Crown Prince then. I was young. I am but thirty now."

"It must be recovered."

"We have tried and failed."

"Your Majesty must pay. It must be bought."

45 "She will not sell."

"Stolen, then."

5 *acquaintance (fml):* Bekanntschaft

5 *adventuress (derog, old-fashioned):* woman who is looking for a rich husband

8 *docket sth. (old-fashioned):* collect and organize sth.

12 *staff-commander:* officer of the Royal Navy

12 *monograph:* lengthy essay on one special subject

17 *become entangled with sb.:* become romantically involved with sb.

25 *produce sth.:* etwas hervorholen

26 *blackmail (n):* Erpressung

29 *pooh:* expression of scorn

29 *forgery:* Fälschung

32 *seal (n):* Siegel

38 *indiscretion:* unwise act

"Five attempts have been made. Twice burglars in my pay ransacked her house. Once we diverted her luggage when she travelled. Twice she has been waylaid. There has been no result."

"No sign of it?"

5 "Absolutely none."

Holmes laughed. "It is quite a pretty little problem," said he.

"But a very serious one to me," returned the King reproachfully.

"Very, indeed. And what does she propose to do with the photograph?"

"To ruin me."

10 "But how?"

"I am about to be married."

"So I have heard."

"To Clotilde Lothman von Saxe-Meningen, second daughter of the King of Scandinavia. You may know the strict principles of her family. She is

15 herself the very soul of delicacy. A shadow of a doubt as to my conduct would bring the matter to an end."

"And Irene Adler?"

"Threatens to send them the photograph. And she will do it. I know that she will do it. You do not know her, but she has a soul of steel. She has the

20 face of the most beautiful of women, and the mind of the most resolute of men. Rather than I should marry another woman, there are no lengths to which she would not go—none."

"You are sure that she has not sent it yet?"

"I am sure."

25 "And why?"

"Because she has said that she would send it on the day when the betrothal was publicly proclaimed. That will be next Monday."

"Oh, then we have three days yet," said Holmes with a yawn. "That is very fortunate, as I have one or two matters of importance to look into just at

30 present. Your Majesty will, of course, stay in London for the present?"

"Certainly. You will find me at the Langham under the name of the Count Von Kramm."

"Then I shall drop you a line to let you know how we progress."

"Pray do so. I shall be all anxiety."

35 "Then, as to money?"

"You have carte blanche."

"Absolutely?"

"I tell you that I would give one of the provinces of my kingdom to have that photograph."

40 "And for present expenses?"

The King took a heavy chamois leather bag from under his cloak and laid it on the table.

"There are three hundred pounds in gold and seven hundred in notes," he said.

45 Holmes scribbled a receipt upon a sheet of his note-book and handed it to him.

"And Mademoiselle's address?" he asked.

1 *burglar:* sb. who breaks into someone's house

1 *ransack sth.:* search sth. (a room etc.) in a hasty and careless way

2 *divert sth.:* etwas umleiten

3 *waylay sb.:* jdn. unterwegs überfallen

7 *reproachful:* vorwurfsvoll

15 *the very soul of delicacy:* die Empfindsamkeit in Person

15 *conduct:* behaviour

21 *there are no lengths to which she would not go:* there is nothing she would not do

27 *betrothal (old-fashioned):* Verlobung

33 *drop sb. a line (infml):* send sb. a message

34 *anxiety* [æŋˈzaɪəti]: fear, nervousness

36 *you have carte blanche:* you can name your price

40 *expenses (pl):* Auslagen, Spesen

41 *chamois* [ˈʃæmi]: kind of leather

45 *receipt* [rɪˈsiːt]: Quittung

"Is Briony Lodge, Serpentine Avenue, St. John's Wood."

Holmes took a note of it. "One other question," said he. "Was the photograph a cabinet?"

"It was."

5   "Then, good-night, your Majesty, and I trust that we shall soon have some good news for you. And good-night, Watson," he added, as the wheels of the royal brougham rolled down the street. "If you will be good enough to call to-morrow afternoon at three o'clock I should like to chat this little matter over with you."

II

10   At three o'clock precisely I was at Baker Street, but Holmes had not yet returned. The landlady informed me that he had left the house shortly after eight o'clock in the morning. I sat down beside the fire, however, with the intention of awaiting him, however long he might be. I was already deeply interested in his inquiry, for, though it was surrounded by none of the grim

15   and strange features which were associated with the two crimes which I have already recorded, still, the nature of the case and the exalted station of his client gave it a character of its own. Indeed, apart from the nature of the investigation which my friend had on hand, there was something in his masterly grasp of a situation, and his keen, incisive reasoning, which made

20   it a pleasure to me to study his system of work, and to follow the quick, subtle methods by which he disentangled the most inextricable mysteries. So accustomed was I to his invariable success that the very possibility of his failing had ceased to enter into my head.

It was close upon four before the door opened, and a drunken-looking

25   groom, ill-kempt and side-whiskered, with an inflamed face and disreputable clothes, walked into the room. Accustomed as I was to my friend's amazing powers in the use of disguises, I had to look three times before I was certain that it was indeed he. With a nod he vanished into the bedroom, whence he emerged in five minutes tweed-suited and respectable, as of old.

30   Putting his hands into his pockets, he stretched out his legs in front of the fire and laughed heartily for some minutes.

"Well, really!" he cried, and then he choked and laughed again until he was obliged to lie back, limp and helpless, in the chair.

"What is it?"

35   "It's quite too funny. I am sure you could never guess how I employed my morning, or what I ended by doing."

"I can't imagine. I suppose that you have been watching the habits, and perhaps the house, of Miss Irene Adler."

"Quite so; but the sequel was rather unusual. I will tell you, however. I left

40   the house a little after eight o'clock this morning in the character of a groom out of work. There is a wonderful sympathy and freemasonry among horsy men. Be one of them, and you will know all that there is to know. I soon found Briony Lodge. It is a *bijou* villa, with a garden at the back, but built out in front right up to the road, two stories. Chubb lock to the door. Large

3 *cabinet:* a cabinet photograph was ca. 10 x 15 cm in size and intended to be put on display in a frame

11 *landlady:* woman from whom one rents a house or room

14 *inquiry:* investigation

14 *grim:* düster

16 *exalted station:* high social status

21 *subtle* ['sʌtl]: subtil, raffiniert

21 *disentangle sth.:* etwas entwirren

21 *inextricable:* verworren

23 *cease:* stop

25 *groom:* servant who looks after horses

25 *ill-kempt:* ungepflegt

25 *side-whiskered:* mit langen Koteletten

25 *inflamed face:* unhealthy red face

25 *disreputable:* not respectable

27 *disguise* [dɪsˈɡaɪz]: Verkleidung

29 *whence:* from where

29 *emerge:* reappear

32 *choke:* sich verschlucken

33 *be obliged to do sth.:* be forced to do sth.

33 *limp:* schlaff

39 *sequel:* sth. that follows sth. else

41 *freemasonry:* allusion to the Freemasons, a secret society

43 *bijou villa:* small but exquisite house

44 *Chubb lock:* brand name of an especially secure door lock, patented 1818

sitting-room on the right side, well furnished, with long windows almost to the floor, and those preposterous English window fasteners which a child could open. Behind there was nothing remarkable, save that the passage window could be reached from the top of the coach-house. I walked round

5   it and examined it closely from every point of view, but without noting anything else of interest.

"I then lounged down the street and found, as I expected, that there was a mews in a lane which runs down by one wall of the garden. I lent the ostlers a hand in rubbing down their horses, and received in exchange

10 twopence, a glass of half-and-half, two fills of shag tobacco, and as much information as I could desire about Miss Adler, to say nothing of half a dozen other people in the neighborhood in whom I was not in the least interested, but whose biographies I was compelled to listen to."

"And what of Irene Adler?" I asked.

15 "Oh, she has turned all the men's heads down in that part. She is the daintiest thing under a bonnet on this planet. So say the Serpentine-mews, to a man. She lives quietly, sings at concerts, drives out at five every day, and returns at seven sharp for dinner. Seldom goes out at other times, except when she sings. Has only one male visitor, but a good deal of him. He is dark,

20 handsome, and dashing, never calls less than once a day, and often twice. He is a Mr. Godfrey Norton, of the Inner Temple. See the advantages of a cabman as a confidant. They had driven him home a dozen times from Serpentine-mews, and knew all about him. When I had listened to all they had to tell, I began to walk up and down near Briony Lodge once more, and

25 to think over my plan of campaign.

"This Godfrey Norton was evidently an important factor in the matter. He was a lawyer. That sounded ominous. What was the relation between them, and what the object of his repeated visits? Was she his client, his friend, or his mistress? If the former, she had probably transferred the photo-

30 graph to his keeping. If the latter, it was less likely. On the issue of this question depended whether I should continue my work at Briony Lodge, or turn my attention to the gentleman's chambers in the Temple. It was a delicate point, and it widened the field of my inquiry. I fear that I bore you with these details, but I have to let you see my little difficulties, if you are to understand

35 the situation."

"I am following you closely," I answered.

"I was still balancing the matter in my mind when a hansom cab drove up to Briony Lodge, and a gentleman sprang out. He was a remarkably handsome man, dark, aquiline, and moustached—evidently the man of whom I

40 had heard. He appeared to be in a great hurry, shouted to the cabman to wait, and brushed past the maid who opened the door with the air of a man who was thoroughly at home.

"He was in the house about half an hour, and I could catch glimpses of him in the windows of the sitting-room, pacing up and down, talking excit-

45 edly, and waving his arms. Of her I could see nothing. Presently he emerged, looking even more flurried than before. As he stepped up to the cab, he pulled a gold watch from his pocket and looked at it earnestly. 'Drive like the

2 *preposterous:* ridiculous

3 *save:* except

3 *passage window:* Flurfenster

7 *lounge (v):* walk in a leisurely manner

8 *mews:* Stallungen

9 *ostler (old-fashioned):* servant who looks after guests' horses

10 *twopence:* small British coin

10 *half-and-half:* drink made from two different kinds of beer

10 *shag tobacco:* loose tobacco

16 *dainty:* zierlich

16 *bonnet:* woman's head covering

20 *dashing (old-fashioned):* self-confident and elegant (used only for men)

21 *Inner Temple:* one of the four Inns of Court, comparable to the 'Anwaltskammer'

22 *confidant* ['kɒnfɪdænt]: source of information

37 *hansom cab:* two-wheeled carriage

39 *aquiline:* having a thin, curved nose

39 *moustached:* einen Schnurrbart tragend

43 *glimpse (n):* brief view

45 *presently:* soon afterwards

46 *flurried:* excited

devil,' he shouted, 'first to Gross & Hankey's in Regent Street, and then to the church of St. Monica in the Edgware Road. Half a guinea if you do it in twenty minutes!'

    "Away they went, and I was just wondering whether I should not do well to follow them when up the lane came a neat little landau, the coachman with his coat only half-buttoned, and his tie under his ear, while all the tags of his harness were sticking out of the buckles. It hadn't pulled up before she shot out of the hall door and into it. I only caught a glimpse of her at the moment, but she was a lovely woman, with a face that a man might die for.

    "'The Church of St. Monica, John,' she cried, 'and half a sovereign if you reach it in twenty minutes.'

    "This was quite too good to lose, Watson. I was just balancing whether I should run for it, or whether I should perch behind her landau when a cab came through the street. The driver looked twice at such a shabby fare, but I jumped in before he could object. 'The Church of St. Monica,' said I, 'and half a sovereign if you reach it in twenty minutes.' It was twenty-five minutes to twelve, and of course it was clear enough what was in the wind.

    "My cabby drove fast. I don't think I ever drove faster, but the others were there before us. The cab and the landau with their steaming horses were in front of the door when I arrived. I paid the man and hurried into the church. There was not a soul there save the two whom I had followed and a surpliced clergyman, who seemed to be expostulating with them. They were all three standing in a knot in front of the altar. I lounged up the side aisle like any other idler who has dropped into a church. Suddenly, to my surprise, the three at the altar faced round to me, and Godfrey Norton came running as hard as he could towards me.

    "Thank God," he cried. "You'll do. Come! Come!"

    "What then?" I asked.

    "Come, man, come, only three minutes, or it won't be legal."

    I was half-dragged up to the altar, and before I knew where I was I found myself mumbling responses which were whispered in my ear, and vouching for things of which I knew nothing, and generally assisting in the secure tying up of Irene Adler, spinster, to Godfrey Norton, bachelor. It was all done in an instant, and there was the gentleman thanking me on the one side and the lady on the other, while the clergyman beamed on me in front. It was the most preposterous position in which I ever found myself in my life, and it was the thought of it that started me laughing just now. It seems that there had been some informality about their license, that the clergyman absolutely refused to marry them without a witness of some sort, and that my lucky appearance saved the bridegroom from having to sally out into the streets in search of a best man. The bride gave me a sovereign, and I mean to wear it on my watch-chain in memory of the occasion."

    "This is a very unexpected turn of affairs," said I; "and what then?"

    "Well, I found my plans very seriously menaced. It looked as if the pair might take an immediate departure, and so necessitate very prompt and energetic measures on my part. At the church door, however, they separated, he driving back to the Temple, and she to her own house. 'I shall drive

---

1 *Gross & Hankey's:* name of a jeweller

5 *landau:* kind of carriage

6 *all the tags of his harness were sticking out of the buckles:* the harness (= Geschirr) hadn't been properly fastened

7 *pull up:* come to a stop

10 *sovereign (n):* gold coin

13 *perch:* ride standing on the back of the carriage

21 *surpliced:* wearing a surplice (= Chorhemd)

22 *clergyman:* member of the clergy (= Klerus)

22 *expostulate:* argue

23 *aisle* [aɪl]: Gang

24 *idler:* someone who has nothing to do

31 *vouch for sth.:* say that sth. is true

33 *spinster:* (usually older) unmarried woman

33 *bachelor:* unmarried man

35 *beam (v):* smile broadly

40 *sally out:* go away in search of sth.

41 *best man:* friend or relative of the bridegroom who assists at the wedding

43 *turn of affairs:* development

44 *menaced:* in danger

45 *necessitate sth.:* make sth. necessary

out in the park at five as usual,' she said as she left him. I heard no more. They drove away in different directions, and I went off to make my own arrangements."

"Which are?"

5   "Some cold beef and a glass of beer," he answered, ringing the bell. "I have been too busy to think of food, and I am likely to be busier still this evening. By the way, Doctor, I shall want your cooperation."

"I shall be delighted."

"You don't mind breaking the law?"

10   "Not in the least."

"Nor running a chance of arrest?"

"Not in a good cause."

"Oh, the cause is excellent!"

"Then I am your man."

15   "I was sure that I might rely on you."

"But what is it you wish?"

"When Mrs. Turner has brought in the tray I will make it clear to you. Now," he said as he turned hungrily on the simple fare that our landlady had provided, "I must discuss it while I eat, for I have not much time. It is nearly

20   five now. In two hours we must be on the scene of action. Miss Irene, or Madame, rather, returns from her drive at seven. We must be at Briony Lodge to meet her."

"And what then?"

"You must leave that to me. I have already arranged what is to occur.

25   There is only one point on which I must insist. You must not interfere, come what may. You understand?"

"I am to be neutral?"

"To do nothing whatever. There will probably be some small unpleasantness. Do not join in it. It will end in my being conveyed into the house. Four

30   or five minutes afterwards the sitting-room window will open. You are to station yourself close to that open window."

"Yes."

"You are to watch me, for I will be visible to you."

"Yes."

35   "And when I raise my hand—so—you will throw into the room what I give you to throw, and will, at the same time, raise the cry of fire. You quite follow me?"

"Entirely."

"It is nothing very formidable," he said, taking a long cigar-shaped roll

40   from his pocket. "It is an ordinary plumber's smoke rocket, fitted with a cap at either end to make it self-lighting. Your task is confined to that. When you raise your cry of fire, it will be taken up by quite a number of people. You may then walk to the end of the street, and I will rejoin you in ten minutes. I hope that I have made myself clear?"

45   "I am to remain neutral, to get near the window, to watch you, and at the signal to throw in this object, then to raise the cry of fire, and to wait you at the corner of the street."

8 *delighted:* very pleased
18 *fare:* food
24 *occur* [əˈkɜː(r)]: happen
29 *convey sb./sth.:* carry sb./ sth.
39 *formidable:* inspiring fear
40 *plumber:* Klempner
40 *smoke rocket:* small cylindrical device that produces smoke; formerly used to locate leaks in pipes
40 *cap:* Zündplättchen
41 *confine sth.:* limit sth.

"Precisely."

"Then you may entirely rely on me."

"That is excellent. I think, perhaps, it is almost time that I prepare for the new role I have to play."

5   He disappeared into his bedroom and returned in a few minutes in the character of an amiable and simple-minded Nonconformist clergyman. His broad black hat, his baggy trousers, his white tie, his sympathetic smile, and general look of peering and benevolent curiosity were such as Mr. John Hare alone could have equalled. It was not merely that Holmes changed his

10   costume. His expression, his manner, his very soul seemed to vary with every fresh part that he assumed. The stage lost a fine actor, even as science lost an acute reasoner, when he became a specialist in crime.

It was a quarter past six when we left Baker Street, and it still wanted ten minutes to the hour when we found ourselves in Serpentine Avenue. It was

15   already dusk, and the lamps were just being lighted as we paced up and down in front of Briony Lodge, waiting for the coming of its occupant. The house was just such as I had pictured it from Sherlock Holmes's succinct description, but the locality appeared to be less private than I expected. On the contrary, for a small street in a quiet neighborhood, it was remarkably

20   animated. There was a group of shabbily dressed men smoking and laughing in a corner, a scissors grinder with his wheel, two guardsmen who were flirting with a nurse-girl, and several well-dressed young men who were lounging up and down with cigars in their mouths.

"You see," remarked Holmes, as we paced to and fro in front of the house,

25   "this marriage rather simplifies matters. The photograph becomes a double-edged weapon now. The chances are that she would be as averse to its being seen by Mr. Godfrey Norton, as our client is to its coming to the eyes of his princess. Now the question is—Where are we to find the photograph?"

"Where, indeed?"

30   "It is most unlikely that she carries it about with her. It is cabinet size. Too large for easy concealment about a woman's dress. She knows that the King is capable of having her waylaid and searched. Two attempts of the sort have already been made. We may take it, then, that she does not carry it about with her."

35   "Where, then?"

"Her banker or her lawyer. There is that double possibility. But I am inclined to think neither. Women are naturally secretive, and they like to do their own secreting. Why should she hand it over to anyone else? She could trust her own guardianship, but she could not tell what indirect or political

40   influence might be brought to bear upon a business man. Besides, remember that she had resolved to use it within a few days. It must be where she can lay her hands upon it. It must be in her own house."

"But it has twice been burgled."

"Pshaw! They did not know how to look."

45   "But how will you look?"

"I will not look."

"What then?"

6 *amiable:* friendly

6 *Nonconformist clergyman:* minister of one of the free churches

8 *benevolent:* wohlwollend

8 *John Hare (1844–1921):* famous Victorian stage actor

12 *acute:* scharfsinnig

16 *occupant:* Bewohner(in)

17 *succinct:* short and exact

21 *scissors grinder:* Scherenschleifer

24 *to and fro:* hin und her

26 *be averse to sth. (fml):* be strongly against sth.

37 *be inclined to do sth.:* geneigt sein, etwas zu tun

39 *guardianship:* Aufsicht

40 *bring sth. to bear on sb.:* put sb. under pressure

41 *resolve to do sth.:* firmly intend to do sth.

44 *pshaw!:* expression of scorn

"I will get her to show me."

"But she will refuse."

"She will not be able to. But I hear the rumble of wheels. It is her carriage. Now carry out my orders to the letter."

5   As he spoke the gleam of the side-lights of a carriage came round the curve of the avenue. It was a smart little landau which rattled up to the door of Briony Lodge. As it pulled up, one of the loafing men at the corner dashed forward to open the door in the hope of earning a copper, but was elbowed away by another loafer, who had rushed up with the same intention. A fierce

10   quarrel broke out, which was increased by the two guardsmen, who took sides with one of the loungers, and by the scissors grinder, who was equally hot upon the other side. A blow was struck, and in an instant the lady, who had stepped from her carriage, was the centre of a little knot of flushed and struggling men, who struck savagely at each other with their fists and sticks.

15   Holmes dashed into the crowd to protect the lady; but just as he reached her he gave a cry and dropped to the ground, with the blood running freely down his face. At his fall the guardsmen took to their heels in one direction and the loungers in the other, while a number of better-dressed people, who had watched the scuffle without taking part in it, crowded in to help the

20   lady and to attend to the injured man. Irene Adler, as I will still call her, had hurried up the steps; but she stood at the top with her superb figure outlined against the lights of the hall, looking back into the street.

"Is the poor gentleman much hurt?" she asked.

"He is dead," cried several voices.

25   "No, no, there's life in him!" shouted another. "But he'll be gone before you can get him to hospital."

"He's a brave fellow," said a woman. "They would have had the lady's purse and watch if it hadn't been for him. They were a gang, and a rough one, too. Ah, he's breathing now."

30   "He can't lie in the street. May we bring him in, marm?"

"Surely. Bring him into the sitting-room. There is a comfortable sofa. This way, please!"

Slowly and solemnly he was borne into Briony Lodge and laid out in the principal room, while I still observed the proceedings from my post by the

35   window. The lamps had been lit, but the blinds had not been drawn, so that I could see Holmes as he lay upon the couch. I do not know whether he was seized with compunction at that moment for the part he was playing, but I know that I never felt more heartily ashamed of myself in my life than when I saw the beautiful creature against whom I was conspiring, or the grace and

40   kindliness with which she waited upon the injured man. And yet it would be the blackest treachery to Holmes to draw back now from the part which he had entrusted to me. I hardened my heart, and took the smoke-rocket from under my ulster. After all, I thought, we are not injuring her. We are but preventing her from injuring another.

45   Holmes had sat up upon the couch, and I saw him motion like a man who is in need of air. A maid rushed across and threw open the window. At the same instant I saw him raise his hand and at the signal I tossed my

2 *refuse sth.:* etwas ablehnen

5 *gleam (n):* Lichtschein

6 *smart:* schick

7 *loaf (v):* hang around doing nothing

8 *copper:* penny

13 *flushed:* red in the face

14 *savage:* wütend

17 *take to one's heels:* run off

19 *scuffle (n):* brief fight

20 *attend to sb./sth.:* sich um jdn./etwas kümmern

30 *marm:* lower-class pronunciation of ma'am (= madam)

33 *solemn:* feierlich

34 *proceedings:* events

37 *seized with compunction:* von Reue ergriffen

39 *conspire:* sich verschwören

39 *grace:* Anstand

40 *wait upon sb.:* sich um jdn. kümmern

41 *treachery* ['tretʃəri]: Verrat

43 *ulster:* kind of coat

45 *motion (v):* make a movement

47 *toss sth.:* throw sth.

rocket into the room with a cry of "Fire!" The word was no sooner out of my mouth than the whole crowd of spectators, well dressed and ill—gentlemen, ostlers, and servant-maids—joined in a general shriek of "Fire!" Thick clouds of smoke curled through the room and out at the open window. I caught a
5 glimpse of rushing figures, and a moment later the voice of Holmes from within assuring them that it was a false alarm. Slipping through the shouting crowd I made my way to the corner of the street, and in ten minutes was rejoiced to find my friend's arm in mine, and to get away from the scene of uproar. He walked swiftly and in silence for some few minutes until we
10 had turned down one of the quiet streets which lead towards the Edgware Road.

"You did it very nicely, Doctor," he remarked. "Nothing could have been better. It is all right."

"You have the photograph?"
15 "I know where it is."

"And how did you find out?"

"She showed me, as I told you she would."

"I am still in the dark."

"I do not wish to make a mystery," said he, laughing. "The matter was
20 perfectly simple. You, of course, saw that everyone in the street was an accomplice. They were all engaged for the evening."

"I guessed as much."

"Then, when the row broke out, I had a little moist red paint in the palm of my hand. I rushed forward, fell down, clapped my hand to my face, and
25 became a piteous spectacle. It is an old trick."

"That also I could fathom."

"Then they carried me in. She was bound to have me in. What else could she do? And into her sitting-room, which was the very room which I suspected. It lay between that and her bedroom, and I was determined to
30 see which. They laid me on a couch, I motioned for air, they were compelled to open the window, and you had your chance."

"How did that help you?"

"It was all-important. When a woman thinks that her house is on fire, her instinct is at once to rush to the thing which she values most. It is a perfectly
35 overpowering impulse, and I have more than once taken advantage of it. In the case of the Darlington Substitution Scandal it was of use to me, and also in the Arnsworth Castle business. A married woman grabs at her baby; an unmarried one reaches for her jewel-box. Now it was clear to me that our lady of to-day had nothing in the house more precious to her than what we
40 are in quest of. She would rush to secure it. The alarm of fire was admirably done. The smoke and shouting were enough to shake nerves of steel. She responded beautifully. The photograph is in a recess behind a sliding panel just above the right bell-pull. She was there in an instant, and I caught a glimpse of it as she half-drew it out. When I cried out that it was a false
45 alarm, she replaced it, glanced at the rocket, rushed from the room, and I have not seen her since. I rose, and, making my excuses, escaped from the house. I hesitated whether to attempt to secure the photograph at once; but

2 *ill:* badly dressed

3 *shriek (n):* loud cry

6 *slip:* move carefully

8 *be rejoiced (old-fashioned):* be very happy

9 *uproar:* noise and confusion

21 *accomplice:* Komplize

23 *row (n)* [raʊ]: fight

23 *moist:* wet

25 *piteous:* mitleiderregend

26 *fathom sth.:* comprehend sth., understand sth.

29 *it lay between:* it was a choice between

40 *quest (n):* search

42 *recess:* opening in a wall

42 *sliding panel:* schiebbare Vertäfelung/Platte

43 *bell-pull:* cord that can be pulled to ring for a servant

the coachman had come in, and as he was watching me narrowly it seemed safer to wait. A little over-precipitance may ruin all."

"And now?" I asked.

"Our quest is practically finished. I shall call with the King to-morrow,
5 and with you, if you care to come with us. We will be shown into the sitting-room to wait for the lady; but it is probable that when she comes she may find neither us nor the photograph. It might be a satisfaction to his Majesty to regain it with his own hands."

"And when will you call?"

10 "At eight in the morning. She will not be up, so that we shall have a clear field. Besides, we must be prompt, for this marriage may mean a complete change in her life and habits. I must wire to the King without delay."

We had reached Baker Street and had stopped at the door. He was searching his pockets for the key when someone passing said:

15 "Good-night, Mister Sherlock Holmes."

There were several people on the pavement at the time, but the greeting appeared to come from a slim youth in an ulster who had hurried by.

"I've heard that voice before," said Holmes, staring down the dimly lit street. "Now, I wonder who the deuce that could have been."

III

20 I slept at Baker Street that night, and we were engaged upon our toast and coffee in the morning when the King of Bohemia rushed into the room.

"You have really got it!" he cried, grasping Sherlock Holmes by either shoulder and looking eagerly into his face.

"Not yet."

25 "But you have hopes?"

"I have hopes."

"Then, come. I am all impatience to be gone."

"We must have a cab."

"No, my brougham is waiting."

30 "Then that will simplify matters." We descended and started off once more for Briony Lodge.

"Irene Adler is married," remarked Holmes.

"Married! When?"

"Yesterday."

35 "But to whom?"

"To an English lawyer named Norton."

"But she could not love him."

"I am in hopes that she does."

"And why in hopes?"

40 "Because it would spare your Majesty all fear of future annoyance. If the lady loves her husband, she does not love your Majesty. If she does not love your Majesty, there is no reason why she should interfere with your Majesty's plan."

2 *over-precipitance (fml):* Übereilung

8 *regain sth.:* get sth. back

12 *wire to sb. (old-fashioned):* send sb. a telegram

17 *slim:* schlank

19 *deuce:* devil

30 *descend:* go down the stairs

"It is true. And yet—Well! I wish she had been of my own station! What a queen she would have made!" He relapsed into a moody silence, which was not broken until we drew up in Serpentine Avenue.

The door of Briony Lodge was open, and an elderly woman stood upon 5 the steps. She watched us with a sardonic eye as we stepped from the brougham.

"Mr. Sherlock Holmes, I believe?" said she.

"I am Mr. Holmes," answered my companion, looking at her with a questioning and rather startled gaze.

10 "Indeed! My mistress told me that you were likely to call. She left this morning with her husband by the 5:15 train from Charing Cross for the Continent."

"What!" Sherlock Holmes staggered back, white with chagrin and surprise. "Do you mean that she has left England?"

15 "Never to return."

"And the papers?" asked the King hoarsely. "All is lost."

"We shall see." He pushed past the servant and rushed into the drawing-room, followed by the King and myself. The furniture was scattered about in every direction, with dismantled shelves and open drawers, as if the lady 20 had hurriedly ransacked them before her flight. Holmes rushed at the bell-pull, tore back a small sliding shutter, and, plunging in his hand, pulled out a photograph and a letter. The photograph was of Irene Adler herself in evening dress, the letter was superscribed to "Sherlock Holmes, Esq. To be left till called for." My friend tore it open and we all three read it together. It 25 was dated at midnight of the preceding night and ran in this way:

MY DEAR MR. SHERLOCK HOLMES,
You really did it very well. You took me in completely. Until after the alarm of fire, I had not a suspicion. But then, when I found how I had betrayed myself, I began to think. I had been warned against you months ago. I had been told that
30 *if the King employed an agent it would certainly be you. And your address had been given me. Yet, with all this, you made me reveal what you wanted to know. Even after I became suspicious, I found it hard to think evil of such a dear, kind old clergyman. But, you know, I have been trained as an actress myself. Male costume is nothing new to me. I often take advantage of the freedom which it*
35 *gives. I sent John, the coachman, to watch you, ran upstairs, got into my walking-clothes, as I call them, and came down just as you departed.*

Well, I followed you to your door, and so made sure that I was really an object of interest to the celebrated Mr. Sherlock Holmes. Then I, rather imprudently, wished you good-night, and started for the Temple to see my husband.
40 *We both thought the best resource was flight, when pursued by so formidable an antagonist; so you will find the nest empty when you call to-morrow. As to the photograph, your client may rest in peace. I love and am loved by a better man than he. The King may do what he will without hindrance from one whom he has cruelly wronged. I keep it only to safeguard myself, and to preserve a*
45 *weapon which will always secure me from any steps which he might take in the*

5 *sardonic:* schadenfroh
12 *the Continent:* Europe
13 *chagrin* [ˈʃægrɪn] *(fml):* displeasure
16 *hoarse:* heiser
19 *dismantle sth.:* take sth. apart
23 *superscribed:* addressed
23 *Esq. = Esquire:* title formerly used instead of Mr.
38 *imprudent:* unwise
40 *resource:* Maßnahme
40 *flight:* Flucht
41 *antagonist:* Gegner

future. I leave a photograph which he might care to possess; and I remain, dear
Mr. Sherlock Holmes,
    Very truly yours,
    IRENE NORTON, née ADLER.

5   "What a woman—oh, what a woman!" cried the King of Bohemia, when we
had all three read this epistle. "Did I not tell you how quick and resolute she
was? Would she not have made an admirable queen? Is it not a pity that she
was not on my level?"

    "From what I have seen of the lady she seems indeed to be on a very
10 different level to your Majesty," said Holmes coldly. "I am sorry that I have
not been able to bring your Majesty's business to a more successful
conclusion."

    "On the contrary, my dear sir," cried the King; "nothing could be more
successful. I know that her word is inviolate. The photograph is now as safe
15 as if it were in the fire."

    "I am glad to hear your Majesty say so."

    "I am immensely indebted to you. Pray tell me in what way I can reward
you. This ring—" He slipped an emerald snake ring from his finger and held
it out upon the palm of his hand.

20   "Your Majesty has something which I should value even more highly,"
said Holmes.

    "You have but to name it."

    "This photograph!"

    The King stared at him in amazement.

25   "Irene's photograph!" he cried. "Certainly, if you wish it."

    "I thank your Majesty. Then there is no more to be done in the matter. I
have the honor to wish you a very good morning." He bowed, and, turning
away without observing the hand which the King had stretched out to him,
he set off in my company for his chambers.

30   And that was how a great scandal threatened to affect the kingdom of
Bohemia, and how the best plans of Mr. Sherlock Holmes were beaten by a
woman's wit. He used to make merry over the cleverness of women, but I
have not heard him do it of late. And when he speaks of Irene Adler, or when
he refers to her photograph, it is always under the honourable title of *the*
35 *woman.*

From: Arthur Conan Doyle, 'A Scandal in Bohemia', The Strand Magazine,
July 1891

4 *née:* geborene

6 *epistle* [ɪ'pɪsl] *(old-fashioned):* letter

14 *inviolate:* incapable of being broken

17 *be indebted to sb.:* jdm. etwas schulden

18 *emerald:* Smaragd

22 *you have but to name it* = you only have to name it

32 *wit:* cleverness

32 *make merry of sth.:* laugh at sth.

Part I:

1 COMPREHENSION Summarize the facts of the 'scandal' in your own words.
   Why does the king seek the help of a private detective?

2 Summarize briefly how Watson describes Holmes's character (p. 5, l. 6 – p. 6, l. 17).

3 Explain the difference between *see* and *observe* according to Holmes (p. 7, ll. 4–15).

4 Look at p. 7, l. 33 – p. 8, l. 13 in which Watson examines the King's note.
   Give more examples of seeing and observing.

What Watson sees	What Watson deduces
What Holmes sees	**What Holmes deduces**

5 'You would certainly have been burned, had you lived a few centuries ago.' (p. 6, l. 27/28)
   Explain what Watson means by this.

6 ANALYSIS Analyse Holmes's behaviour toward his royal guest.
   What does it show us about Holmes and his character?

Part II:

7 COMPREHENSION Outline the events of Part II in chronological order.

8 ANALYSIS In Part II Holmes displays one of his other talents.
   Give examples from the text and explain why this talent is useful in Holmes's job.

Part III:

9 Watson emphasizes Holmes's admiration of Irene Adler twice in the story.
   Speculate on reasons for his admiration, giving examples from the text.

10 SPEAKING Choose one of the following tasks.
    Doyle's Sherlock Holmes stories were, and still are, enormously popular worldwide.
    Make notes on possible reasons for this popularity. Then explain them in a short talk to the class.
    OR
    Make a short statement explaining why you do not like this kind of fiction.

11 MEDIATION You are preparing a presentation on the secondary character Dr. Watson. With the help of the following essay, write a text of about 170 words describing Watson's relationship to Holmes.

Man mag es kaum glauben, aber ein paarmal hat er sich tatsächlich selber als Detektiv versucht. Das war in der trüben Zeit zwischen 1891 und 1894, als er seinen bewunderten Freund Sherlock Holmes für tot halten mußte — umgekommen in den Klippen der Reichenbachfälle. Doch so sehr er sein
5 Hirn auch strapazierte, um „die Methoden" fachgerecht anzuwenden, die er im Lauf der zehnjährigen, na ja, Zusammenarbeit mit dem Genius der Kriminalistik kennengelernt hatte, der Erfolg blieb mager.

Es läßt sich eben nicht verschweigen: Dr. med. John Watson, der wackere Praktikus und vorbildliche Normalbrite, ist und bleibt ein Vertreter des
10 gesunden Menschenverstands und — des schönen Anstandsgefühls. Das ästhetische Vergnügen an der Dramaturgie des Verbrechens geht ihm ebenso wider die Natur wie das kühl berechnende Deduzieren à la Holmes. Ihm fehlt einfach das Elementare. Wie oft hat ihm Holmes nicht gepredigt: „Sie sehen dasselbe wie ich, aber Sie beobachten nicht!"
15 Darum war Dr. Watson, der 1878 an der Universität London promovierte Ex-Militärarzt der Britischen Armee in Indien, auch doppelt froh, als Holmes so unvermutet (und wie üblich undurchschaubar verkleidet) wieder aufkreuzte und ihm den Fall des „Leeren Hauses" abnahm: Die eigenständige Detektivlaufbahn war definitiv zu Ende, und er konnte auf seinen ange-
20 stammten Platz zurückkehren. Es ist der Platz im Schatten des Großen, worüber sich Watson aber nie ernstlich beklagt hat. Er dient halt als „Sturmvogel des Verbrechens", wie Holmes ihn einmal ironisch titulierte, als Durchschnittdenker, der mit seinen raschen und naheliegenden, doch stets unrettbar hakenden Ansichten den (Widerspruchs-)Geist des Partners erst
25 so richtig befeuert.

Doch mag das alles so sein. Mag Holmes während ihrer gemeinsamen Jahre in Baker Street 221B sogar das Scheckbuch des leichtlebigen und immer noch recht jungen Kolonialoffiziers a.D. verwaltet haben (als man die Räumlichkeiten der guten Mrs. Hudson bezog, war der 1852 geborene
30 Watson gerade 29 Jahre alt) — in einem ist Dr. Watson denn doch der Überlegene: Er ist der weitaus bessere Erzähler, so gern der Meister über die „reißerische" Schreibtechnik seines Chronisten lästerte und sich lieber eine „wissenschaftliche" Deskription seiner Taten gewünscht hätte —als Holmes, im späten „Buch der Fälle", höchstselbst über einige seiner Ermittlungen
35 referierte, geriet das Resultat eher dünn.

Nein, es kann nicht bestritten werden: Sherlock Holmes ist ohne Dr. Watson undenkbar. Die legendäre Erstbegegnung der beiden im Londoner St. Bartholomew's Hospital („You have been in Afghanistan, I perceive"), die Dr. Watson im autobiographischen Einleitungskapitel der „Studie in Schar-
40 lachrot" beschreibt, sie ist für den Ruhm des angehenden „Consulting detective" nicht weniger bedeutsam geworden als für das Schicksal seines künftigen Boswell/Eckermann. (Und wie gut, daß Dr. Watson kurz darauf den Medizinerkollegen und Schriftkundigen Arthur Conan Doyle kennengelernt hat).

42 *Boswell, Eckermann:* biographers of famous men

Schön auch, daß die so ungleiche Partnerschaft zwischen Holmes und Watson, dem Genie und dem Mann des Common Sense, standgehalten hat, als Freund Watson die Wohngemeinschaft verließ, um die hübsche Mary Morstan zu heiraten („nun, Watson, das schöne Geschlecht fällt in Ihr Fach") und in Paddington eine Praxis zu eröffnen. Und wenn der leidgeprüfte Adlatus wirklich einmal an seiner detektivischen Begrenztheit litt, gab es da ja einen, der noch wesentlich beschränkter und begriffsstutziger war als er: Inspector Lestrade von Scotland Yard. Ein dauerhafter Trost für alle Watsons.

Aber eigentlich braucht er keinen Trost. Er hat sich als Chronist und Kontrastfigur absolut unentbehrlich gemacht. Als Vorbild aller künftigen Kriminalassistenten, von Captain Hastings bis Archie Goodwin. Sein — bescheidener — Platz in der literarischen Ewigkeit ist ihm gewiß. Ein Denkmal für Dr. Watson? Nicht nötig: „Monumentum quaeris — lege."

From: Heiko Postma, 'John Watson, M. D. von Arthur Conan Doyle', Galerie der Detektive. 123 Portraits von Sherlock Holmes bis Nero Wolfe, *1997*

12 *Captain Arthur Hastings:* companion of detective Hercule Poirot in the works of Agatha Christie

12 *Archie Goodwin:* assistant of detective Nero Wolfe and narrator of Rex Stout's mystery novels

14 *Monumentum quaeris — lege (Lat.):* You seek my monument? Read!

INFOBOX	**Arthur Conan Doyle**

Arthur Conan Doyle (1859–1930) was born in Edinburgh, the son of Irish Catholic parents. His father was a moderately successful artist, but also a chronic alcoholic; his mother was a gifted story-teller. With the support of wealthier relatives Doyle attended boarding school and later university, where he studied medicine. After a time as a ship's doctor Doyle settled down in Portsmouth and set up practice. However, he found it difficult to earn a living with medicine. Since his student days Doyle had written stories on the side, some of which were published. His fortunes changed with the publication of his first Sherlock Holmes story, A Study in Scarlet (1887). Numerous stories featuring the master detective and his faithful companion, Dr Watson, made Doyle wealthy and brought him international popularity. All in all Doyle wrote 60 Sherlock Holmes stories, including four novels. Doyle is also the author of several historical novels as well as non-fiction.

2 Sherlock – A Scandal in Belgravia

A Scandal in Belgravia *is the fourth episode of the BBC series* Sherlock *and was first broadcast 1 January 2012. It is based loosely on Doyle's story* 'A Scandal in Bohemia'.

title *Belgravia:* fashionable district of Central London

1a *dominatrix* [ˌdɒmɪˈneɪtrɪks]: female sex worker who plays the dominant role in sadomasochistic practices

in the film *Coventry:* British city that was severely damaged by German bombs in WWII

MOD: *Ministry of Defence*

The story

1 a VIEWING In the TV episode, the dominatrix Irene Adler has a mobile phone that plays an important role in the plot. While you are watching the episode, track her phone as it moves through the story. Add the missing information to the table.

	Where	Who	What
1	Buckingham Palace	Sherlock, Watson, Mycroft, representative of the Royal Family	
2	house in Belgravia	Adler, Holmes, Watson, CIA agents	
3	221B Baker Street	Mrs Hudson, Watson, Holmes, party guests	
4	221B Baker Street	Holmes, Mrs Hudson, CIA agent	
5	morgue	Holmes, Molly Hooper (pathologist)	
6	221B Baker Street	Holmes, Watson, Adler	
7	hotel room	Adler, S. Holmes, M. Holmes	
8	221B Baker Street	Holmes, Watson	

b COMPREHENSION Use the notes you have made to explain the plot to your partner. Discuss any points on which you disagree or of which you are unsure.

2   a   Choose one of the following tasks.

The makers of the TV series *Sherlock* transported the hero from Victorian England to the 21st century. Outline ways in which the figure of Sherlock Holmes has been adapted to the modern age.
OR
While the TV adaptation is very different from Doyle's story 'A Scandal in Bohemia', it also alludes to the original in several places. List some of these allusions.

    b   Find three students who have chosen the same task. Compare your results in your group and prepare a short presentation for your class.

The characters

3   ANALYSIS Examine the relationship between Sherlock Holmes and Irene Adler in the TV episode, pointing out examples.

4   a   Examine Benedict Cumberbatch's interpretation of the famous detective. Together with a partner, make notes on the impression he creates: his speech, his behaviour, his relationships to other people etc.. Add examples from the TV series.

    b   Write a text of about 200 words in which you describe Holmes's character as he appears in the TV series.

Film technique

5   a   Examine the excerpt 13:17 – 13:47 and describe the techniques used to make Holmes's process of observation and deduction visible for the viewer.

    b   A jump cut is a sudden cut from one setting to another, usually to alternate between two different sets of characters. Examine the use of jump cuts in the excerpt 18:45 – 19:13. Analyse the effect they have on the viewer.

Sherlock 2.0

6   Read the following excerpt from Alyssa Rosenberg's review of the BBC series. Comment on Rosenberg's view of the modernity of the Sherlock figure.

In a sense, Holmes is perfectly suited for life in the Internet age, an era when specialized, obsessive knowledge makes the fanboy, or policy blogger, king. Holmes' monographs on cigar ash may be less strange today than they would have been to Victorian readers, but that's only because it's easier to form communities around obscure interests and information than it used to be. We live in a time when knowledge doesn't have to be inherently and regularly useful to bind people together. As Holmes, Benedict Cumberbatch is a wonderful whip-thin, Aspergerian, asexual type, like Sheldon on The Big Bang Theory but with more charisma. With his multiple fascinations and expertise, his disinterest in men or women or anything unrelated to his work, Holmes is no longer an occasionally necessary Victorian oddity. He's king of the modern nerds.

From: Alyssa Rosenberg, 'Sherlock Holmes Meets the 21st Century', The Atlantic, 19 Oct. 2010.

7   **LISTENING** SPT352388-27 Listen to a podcast from National Public Radio marking the US premiere of the BBC series. Read sentences 1–10 before you listen to the text. Complete them while you listen to the podcast.

1   The presenter, Linda Wertheimer, says that Doyle's famous detective is an earlier version of today's

   ....

2   One of the interview partners, Steven Moffat, is one of the two people who ....

   ....

3   Moffat has been a fan of Holmes stories since ....

4   Moffat says that he and Mark Gatiss liked the Basil Rathbone film versions of Doyle's stories

   because the plots were ....

5   As an example of a parallel between Doyle's stories and the modern TV series, Moffat points out

   that the original Watson kept a .... , whereas the modern Watson

   ....

6   Moffat is sure that if Sherlock Holmes lived today, he would ....

   ....

7   Cumberbatch says that to learn how to act the part of Holmes you must ....

   ....

8   According to Wertheimer, in the films starring Basil Rathbone as Holmes, Watson is represented as

   ....

9   Moffat and Cumberbatch agree that the bond between Holmes and Watson is based on

   ....

10 Cumberbatch says that when Holmes thinks out loud it has to ....

   ....

Literature and film

8   a   Which do you prefer, Doyle's story or the TV adaptation?
       Brainstorm your reasons and write them down.

   b   Discuss the advantages of each format – the written story and the film version – in class.

3 The Tell-Tale Heart

EDGAR ALLAN POE

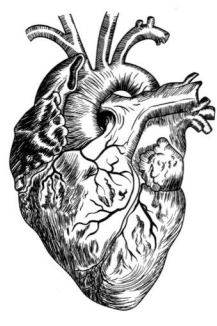

The following story was first published in 1843. It belongs to the genre of Gothic fiction which centres on themes of passion and madness, often in a bleak or mysterous setting.

TRUE!—nervous—very, very dreadfully nervous I had been and am; but
5 why *will* you say that I am mad? The disease had sharpened my senses—not destroyed—not dulled them. Above all was the sense of hearing acute. I heard all things in the heaven and in the earth. I heard many things in hell. How, then, am I mad? Hearken! and observe how healthily—how calmly I can tell you the whole story.

10 It is impossible to say how first the idea entered my brain; but once conceived, it haunted me day and night. Object there was none. Passion there was none. I loved the old man. He had never wronged me. He had never given me insult. For his gold I had no desire. I think it was his eye! yes, it was this! He had the eye of a vulture—a pale blue eye, with a film over it.
15 Whenever it fell upon me, my blood ran cold; and so by degrees—very gradually—I made up my mind to take the life of the old man, and thus rid myself of the eye forever.

Now this is the point. You fancy me mad. Madmen know nothing. But you should have seen *me*. You should have seen how wisely I proceeded—
20 with what caution—with what foresight—with what dissimulation I went to work! I was never kinder to the old man than during the whole week before I killed him. And every night, about midnight, I turned the latch of his door and opened it—oh, so gently! And then, when I had made an opening sufficient for my head, I put in a dark lantern, all closed, closed, that no light
25 shone out, and then I thrust in my head. Oh, you would have laughed to see how cunningly I thrust it in! I moved it slowly—very, very slowly, so that I might not disturb the old man's sleep. It took me an hour to place my whole head within the opening so far that I could see him as he lay upon his bed. Ha!—would a madman have been so wise as this? And then, when my head
30 was well in the room, I undid the lantern cautiously—oh, so cautiously—cautiously (for the hinges creaked)—I undid it just so much that a single thin ray fell upon the vulture eye. And this I did for seven long nights—every night just at midnight—but I found the eye always closed; and so it was impossible to do the work; for it was not the old man who vexed me, but his
35 Evil Eye. And every morning, when the day broke, I went boldly into the chamber, and spoke courageously to him, calling him by name in a hearty tone, and inquiring how he has passed the night. So you see he would have been a very profound old man, indeed, to suspect that every night, just at twelve, I looked in upon him while he slept.

40 Upon the eighth night I was more than usually cautious in opening the door. A watch's minute hand moves more quickly than did mine. Never before that night had I *felt the* extent of my own powers—of my sagacity. I

title *tell-tale:* verräterisch (tale = story)

6 *dull sth. (v):* etwas abstumpfen

6 *acute:* sharp

8 *hearken* ['hɑːrkən] (old-fashioned): listen

11 *conceive sth.:* (einen Gedanken usw.) fassen

11 *haunt sb.:* follow sb. in a troubling way

11 *object:* purpose

14 *vulture:* Geier

18 *you fancy me mad:* you think that I am crazy

19 *proceed:* continue, progress

20 *caution:* carefulness

20 *with foresight:* vorausschauend

20 *dissimulation:* ability to hide your real intentions

24 *dark lantern:* abgedunkelte Laterne

25 *thrust sth. into sth.:* etwas in etwas hineinstoßen

26 *cunning (adj):* clever

31 *hinge:* Scharnier

34 *vex sb.:* make sb. angry

35 *Evil Eye:* in earlier times people who had the 'evil eye' were thought to be able to harm others by looking at them (= der 'böse Blick')

35 *bold:* brave, confident

38 *profound:* tiefsinnig

42 *extent:* Ausmaß

42 *sagacity* [sə'gæsəti]: cleverness

could scarcely contain my feelings of triumph. To think that there I was, opening the door, little by little, and he not even to dream of my secret deeds or thoughts. I fairly chuckled at the idea; and perhaps he heard me; for he moved on the bed suddenly, as if startled. Now you may think that I drew
5 back—but no. His room was as black as pitch with the thick darkness (for the shutters were close fastened, through fear of robbers), and so I knew that he could not see the opening of the door, and I kept pushing it on steadily, steadily.

I had my head in, and was about to open the lantern, when my thumb
10 slipped upon the tin fastening, and the old man sprang up in bed, crying out—"Who's there?"

I kept quite still and said nothing. For a whole hour I did not move a muscle, and in the meantime I did not hear him lie down. He was still sitting up in the bed listening;—just as I have done, night after night, hearkening to
15 the death watches in the wall.

Presently I heard a slight groan, and I knew it was the groan of mortal terror. It was not a groan of pain or of grief—oh, no!—it was the low stifled sound that arises from the bottom of the soul when overcharged with awe. I knew the sound well. Many a night, just at midnight, when all the world
20 slept, it has welled up from my own bosom, deepening, with its dreadful echo, the terrors that distracted me. I say I knew it well. I knew what the old man felt, and pitied him, although I chuckled at heart. I knew that he had been lying awake ever since the first slight noise, when he had turned in the bed. His fears had been ever since growing upon him. He had been trying to
25 fancy them causeless, but could not. He had been saying to himself—"It is nothing but the wind in the chimney—it is only a mouse crossing the floor," or "It is merely a cricket which has made a single chirp." Yes, he had been trying to comfort himself with these suppositions: but he had found all in vain. *All in vain;* because Death, in approaching him had stalked with his
30 black shadow before him, and enveloped the victim. And it was the mournful influence of the unperceived shadow that caused him to feel—although he neither saw nor heard—to *feel* the presence of my head within the room.

When I had waited a long time, very patiently, without hearing him lie down, I resolved to open a little—a very, very little crevice in the lantern. So
35 I opened it—you cannot imagine how stealthily, stealthily—until, at length a single dim ray, like the thread of the spider, shot from out the crevice and fell full upon the vulture eye.

It was open—wide, wide open—and I grew furious as I gazed upon it. I saw it with perfect distinctness—all a dull blue, with a hideous veil over it
40 that chilled the very marrow in my bones; but I could see nothing else of the old man's face or person: for I had directed the ray, as if by instinct, precisely upon the damned spot.

And have I not told you that what you mistake for madness is but over-acuteness of the senses?—now, I say, there came to my ears a low, dull, quick
45 sound, such as a watch makes when enveloped in cotton. I knew *that* sound well, too. It was the beating of the old man's heart. It increased my fury, as the beating of a drum stimulates the soldier into courage.

3 *I fairly chuckled:* I had to laugh
4 *startle sb.:* surprise or shock sb. suddenly
6 *shutter:* Fensterladen
10 *tin fastening:* Blechverschluss
15 *death watch:* beetle that lives in the wooden walls of old houses. Its knocking sound was said to predict sb.'s death.
16 *groan (n):* cry of pain
16 *mortal terror:* Todesangst
17 *stifled:* gedämpft
18 *awe:* Ehrfurcht
20 *well up:* emporquellen
27 *cricket:* Grille
28 *supposition:* Annahme
28 *in vain:* umsonst, vergeblich
30 *mournful:* very sad
31 *unperceived:* unseen
34 *resolve sth.:* decide sth.
34 *crevice* ['krevɪs]: Spalt
35 *stealthy:* unmerklich
38 *furious:* extremely angry
38 *gaze (v):* look closely
39 *hideous:* horrible
40 *marrow:* Knochenmark

But even yet I refrained and kept still. I scarcely breathed. I held the lantern motionless. I tried how steadily I could maintain the ray upon the eve. Meantime the hellish tattoo of the heart increased. It grew quicker and quicker, and louder and louder every instant. The old man's terror *must* have
5   been extreme! It grew louder, I say, louder every moment!—do you mark me well? I have told you that I am nervous: so I am. And now at the dead hour of the night, amid the dreadful silence of that old house, so strange a noise as this excited me to uncontrollable terror. Yet, for some minutes longer I refrained and stood still. But the beating grew louder, louder! I thought the
10   heart must burst. And now a new anxiety seized me—the sound would be heard by a neighbor! The old man's hour had come! With a loud yell, I threw open the lantern and leaped into the room. He shrieked once—once only. In an instant I dragged him to the floor, and pulled the heavy bed over him. I then smiled gaily, to find the deed so far done. But, for many minutes, the
15   heart beat on with a muffled sound. This, however, did not vex me; it would not be heard through the wall. At length it ceased. The old man was dead. I removed the bed and examined the corpse. Yes, he was stone, stone dead. I placed my hand upon the heart and held it there many minutes. There was no pulsation. He was stone dead. His eye would trouble me no more.
20   If still you think me mad, you will think so no longer when I describe the wise precautions I took for the concealment of the body. The night waned, and I worked hastily, but in silence. First of all I dismembered the corpse. I cut off the head and the arms and the legs.
         I then took up three planks from the flooring of the chamber, and depos-
25   ited all between the scantlings. I then replaced the boards so cleverly, so cunningly, that no human eye—not even his—could have detected anything wrong. There was nothing to wash out—no stain of any kind—no blood-spot whatever. I had been too wary for that. A tub had caught all—ha! ha!
         When I had made an end of these labors, it was four o'clock—still dark as
30   midnight. As the bell sounded the hour, there came a knocking at the street door. I went down to open it with a light heart,—for what had I *now* to fear? There entered three men, who introduced themselves, with perfect suavity, as officers of the police. A shriek had been heard by a neighbour during the night; suspicion of foul play had been aroused; information had been lodged
35   at the police office, and they (the officers) had been deputed to search the premises.
         I smiled,—for *what* had I to fear? I bade the gentlemen welcome. The shriek, I said, was my own in a dream. The old man, I mentioned, was absent in the country. I took my visitors all over the house. I bade them search—
40   search *well*. I led them, at length, to *his* chamber. I showed them his treasures, secure, undisturbed. In the enthusiasm of my confidence, I brought chairs into the room, and desired them *here* to rest from their fatigues, while I myself, in the wild audacity of my perfect triumph, placed my own seat upon the very spot beneath which reposed the corpse of the victim.
45   The officers were satisfied. My *manner* had convinced them. I was singularly at ease. They sat, and while I answered cheerily, they chatted of familiar things. But, ere long, I felt myself getting pale and wished them gone. My

1 *refrain:* hold back, take no action

3 *tattoo:* beating sound

5 *mark sb. (old-fashioned):* pay attention to sb.

10 *anxiety* [æŋˈzaɪəti]: fear

10 *seize sb.* [siːz] : take/grab sb.

12 *shriek (v):* cry, scream

14 *gay:* happy

15 *muffled:* gedämpft

16 *cease:* stop

21 *concealment:* act of hiding sth.

21 *wane:* come to an end

25 *scantling:* Balken

28 *wary:* cautious

32 *suavity:* elegant/polite/confident manner

34 *suspicion:* Verdacht

34 *arouse sth.:* etwas erregen

34 *lodge sth.:* etwas deponieren

35 *depute sb. (fml):* jdn. abordnen

36 *premises (pl.):* house/apartment

42 *fatigue:* tiring work

43 *audacity:* Kühnheit

45 *singularly:* completely

46 *at ease:* relaxed

47 *ere (old-fashioned):* before

head ached, and I fancied a ringing in my ears: but still they sat and still chatted. The ringing became more distinct:—it continued and became more distinct: I talked more freely to get rid of the feeling: but it continued and gained definiteness—until, at length, I found that the noise was not within
5 my ears.

No doubt I now grew very pale;—but I talked more fluently, and with a heightened voice. Yet the sound increased—and what could I do? It was *a low, dull, quick sound—much such a sound as a watch makes when enveloped in cotton.* I gasped for breath—and yet the officers heard it not. I talked more
10 quickly —more vehemently; but the noise steadily increased. I arose and argued about trifles, in a high key and with violent gesticulations; but the noise steadily increased. Why would they not be gone? I paced the floor to and fro with heavy strides, as if excited to fury by the observations of the men —but the noise steadily increased. Oh God! what *could* I do? I foamed—
15 I raved—I swore! I swung the chair upon which I had been sitting, and grated it upon the boards, but the noise arose over all and continually increased. It grew louder—louder—*louder!* And still the men chatted pleasantly, and smiled. Was it possible they heard not? Almighty God!—no, no! They heard!—they suspected!—they knew!—they were making a mockery of my
20 horror!—this I thought, and this I think. But anything was better than this agony! Anything was more tolerable than this derision! I could bear those hypocritical smiles no longer! I felt that I must scream or die! and now— again!—hark! louder! louder! louder! *louder!*

"Villains!" I shrieked, "dissemble no more! I admit the deed!—tear up the
25 planks! here, here! – it is the beating of his hideous heart!"

From: Edgar Allan Poe, 'The Tell-Tale Heart', The Pioneer, January 1843

11 *trifle:* sth. unimportant
11 *key:* Tonart
13 *stride:* step
14 *foam (v):* schäumen
15 *rave:* toben
15 *grate sth.:* drag sth. so that it makes an unpleasant noise
19 *make a mockery of sth.:* make fun of sth.
21 *agony:* extreme pain
21 *derision:* Hohn
22 *hypocritical:* heuchlerisch
23 *hark! (old-fashioned):* listen!
24 *villain:* Bösewicht
24 *dissemble:* heucheln

1 **COMPREHENSION** Summarize the events of the plot — as the narrator presents them — in a few sentences.

ANALYSIS **The Plot**

2 a Draw a diagram showing how the suspense rises and falls in the course of the story. Mark important events in the plot in key words on your chart.

b Compare diagrams with a partner. Discuss the reasons for your choices.

3 a Analyse how the protagonist represents the relationship between himself and the reader in the opening paragraph of the story (ll. 4–9).

b Work with a partner. Analyse the first three paragraphs of the text (ll. 4–39).
Partner A collects the evidence the narrator presents to prove his sanity.
Partner B collects evidence that the narrator is a 'madman'. Then compare your results.

c Write a short text (150 words) on the impression the narrator makes on the reader. Give examples from the text.

4 Examine the language Poe uses in the climatic paragraph of the text (ll. 7–24).

a Look for examples of these rhetorical devices:
antithesis – exclamation – asyndeton – repetition – parallelism – climax

b Analyse how the author uses them to convey an impression of his narrator's mental state.

5 We speak of *situational irony* when a situation proves to be the opposite of what it at first appears to be. An example: someone misses their plane and then learns that the plane has crashed. In groups, discuss whether the term *situational irony* can be applied to the conclusion of the story.

6 A typical theme in detective stories is the 'perfect crime'. Explain how Poe employs this theme and at the same time destroys it.

7 **WRITING** Poe's story is told by a man who may be insane.
Choose one of the following and use it as a basis for an interpretation of the text (300 words):

> The story is about a mentally disturbed individual who murders a harmless old man for no reason. His guilty conscience drives him to confess.
> OR
> The story is about a psychotic who has completely lost contact with reality. He imagines that he commits a murder, then he imagines that the police come for him.
> OR
> The narrator suffers from a split personality. He tries to rid himself of his other self, but in the end he fails.

8 **MEDIATION** Your American friend recently read that Poe's literary reputation is much higher in Europe than it is in the USA, and asks you if you have any information on this topic. You find the following interview with a German expert on Poe. Outline the relevant information in an email reply to your friend.

Der Anglist und Biograf Hans-Dieter Gelfert, 72, über Edgar Allan Poe und die Schönheit des Schreckens

SPIEGEL: Der Geburtstag von Edgar Allan Poe jährt sich jetzt zum 200. Mal – seine Fangemeinde reicht von Kafka, Stalin und Hitchcock bis zum
5 Schock-Rocker Marilyn Manson. In Berlin wird im März ein neues Poe-Musical uraufgeführt. Woher rührt die Begeisterung für den düsteren Klassiker?

GELFERT: Poes Geschichten zielen darauf, eine geistige Gänsehaut hervorzurufen. Auf intellektueller Ebene muss man ihn als den wohl meistgele-
10 senen und vielseitigsten amerikanischen Klassiker würdigen. Poe war Lyriker, Erzähler, Kritiker und Philosoph, auf all diesen Gebieten war er ein Anreger und blieb bis heute lebendig.

SPIEGEL: Poe gilt als Meister des Morbiden, viele seiner Erzähler sind feingeistige Psychopathen, sein poetisches Lieblingsthema ist der Tod schöner
15 Frauen. War er deshalb in seiner amerikanischen Heimat lange nicht als Klassiker anerkannt?

GELFERT: In den USA werden die Lobeshymnen auch jetzt eher gedämpft ausfallen. Es geht bei Poe nicht um Moral. Das ist es, was die amerikanischen Leser abschreckt. Als Verächter der Demokratie und jemand, der die
20 Sklaverei billigte, war er dort politisch nie akzeptabel, und dann noch seine Trunksucht und die Ehe mit einem 13-jährigen Mädchen - das alles machte ihn suspekt. Poe ist Amerikas ungeliebter Klassiker. Umso mehr liebten ihn die Europäer.

SPIEGEL: Charles Baudelaire gilt als Poes europäischer Entdecker.
25 GELFERT: Baudelaire, der sich ja selbst als Bürgerschreck aufführte, sah in Poe ein frühes Abbild seiner selbst. Während in Amerika im 19. Jahrhundert der Puritanismus eine Hochphase erlebte, war in Europa schon die Emanzipation des Individuums von den Zwängen der Gesellschaft das moderne künstlerische Motiv.

30 SPIEGEL: Die Abgründe der Seele, das Irrationale stehen bei Poe im Zentrum. Gleichzeitig löst sein Detektiv Dupin seine Fälle durch scharfsinnige, logische Analyse.

GELFERT: Ohne Dupin wäre Sherlock Holmes nicht denkbar. In den Detektivgeschichten wird gerade das Rationale ins Extrem getrieben. Es geht bei
35 Poe aber nicht um aufgeklärte Vernunft. Für ihn liegt das Entscheidende jenseits der Ratio, nämlich im Willen. In seinem wichtigen Essay „Heureka" vermutet Poe sogar, nach dem Menschen könne der Übermensch kommen. Nietzsche, der Poe sehr schätzte, hat in ihm offenbar eine innere Verwandtschaft gespürt. Poes Weltsicht ist jenseits von Gut und Böse. Die Kunst soll
40 Schönheit hervorbringen, auch die Schönheit des Schreckens.

From: Der Spiegel, *4/2009*

24 *Charles Baudelaire (1821–1867):* French poet, translated the works of Poe into French

31 *Dupin:* detective-hero of Poe's story 'The Murders in the Rue Morgue'

38 *Friedrich Nietzsche (1844–1900):* German philosopher

4 The Open Window  SPT352388-34

H. H. MUNRO

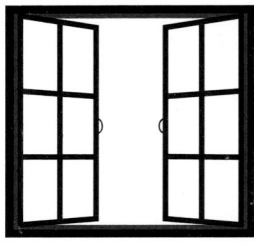

The story you will hear is a hair-raising yet funny short fiction from 1930.

1 Before you listen to the text, look at these words which will help you understand it:

> **self-possessed:** *self-confident* – **endeavour:** *try* – **mope:** *feel sorry for yourself* –
> **communion:** *conversation* – **french window:** *Terrassenfenster* – **snipe:** *Schnepfe (ein Vogel)* –
> **be engulfed:** *versinken* – **treacherous:** *tückisch* – **bog:** *wet ground* – **bustle:** *move noisily* –
> **briskly:** *energisch* – **scarcity:** *Knappheit* – **ghastly:** *grauenerregend* – **labour (v):** *suffer* –
> **ailment:** *illness* – **headlong:** *überstürzt* – **bolt:** *run in panic* – **cemetery:** *graveyard* –
> **pariah dog:** *wild dog* – **romance:** *story* – **at short notice:** *without time for preparation*

2 **LISTENING** Read the sentences below. Then listen to the story and complete the statements below with information from the text. Write no more than 5–6 words for each answer.

1 The niece is .... years old.

2 Nuttel is suffering from bad ....

3 Nuttel was given a letter of introduction by ....

4 Nuttel's sister stayed in the area .... years ago.

5 The hunting accident the girl tells Nuttel about happened .... ago.

6 In the accident .... were lost.

7 The niece tells Nuttel that the bodies of the men ....

8 When Mrs Sappleton appears, she tells Nuttel that she is expecting ....
....

9 When Nuttel sees the look of horror on the girl's face, he ....

10 When a voice starts to sing, Nuttel ....

11 The three figures coming across the lawn are ....

12 Vera explains Nuttel's sudden departure by saying that he is ....

3 a ANALYSIS Listen to the story again. Tick the item that you think best completes each statement:

1 Framton Nuttel has come to the Sappletons because …

☐ his sister told him to go there.
☐ he hopes Mrs Sappleton will help him.
☐ he is lonely.

2 Vera tells him a story about a terrible accident that happened to her family because …

☐ she wants to entertain him.
☐ she wants to see what happens.
☐ she wants to prepare him for her aunt's mental state.

3 Mrs Sappleton watches the open window closely because …

☐ she is bored by Nuttel's stories.
☐ she believes in ghosts.
☐ she expects her husband and her brothers to return.

4 Nuttel runs off in panic when he sees the three men coming because …

☐ he thinks they are ghosts.
☐ he doesn't want to meet them.
☐ he is afraid of dogs.

5 Mrs Sappleton thinks that Nuttel's behaviour …

☐ was caused by his bad nerves.
☐ is quite impolite.
☐ is connected with a ghost story.

6 Vera tells the others the story about Nuttel's experience in India because …

☐ she enjoys making up hair-raising stories.
☐ she wants to excuse Nuttel's behaviour.
☐ Nuttel had told her about his horrible experience earlier.

b Compare answers with your partner. Discuss the items you disagree on.
If necessary, listen to the story again.

INFOBOX	H. H. Munro

Hector Hugh Monro was born in 1870 in Burma (today Myanmar), at that time a British colony. His father, an Inspector General for the Indian Imperial Police, sent his son to Britain, where he was brought up by his grandmother and aunts. As a young man he rejoined his father on the police force in Burma, but returned to Britain after two years and took up work as a journalist. At the outbreak of World War I he volunteered for service and was killed in battle in 1916. He is best known for his short stories, which appeared under the pen name 'Saki'.

5 The Birds

DAPHNE DU MAURIER

In the following story from 1952, mysterious things happen in a seemingly quiet and peaceful corner of Cornwall.

1 While you are reading the story, keep a kind of diary in which you list Nat Hocken's observations and experiences for each day.

On December the third the wind changed overnight and it was winter. Until then the autumn had been mellow, soft. The leaves had lingered on the trees, golden red, and the hedgerows were still green. The earth was rich where the plough had turned it.

5   Nat Hocken, because of a war-time disability, had a pension and did not work full-time at the farm. He worked three days a week, and they gave him the lighter jobs: hedging, thatching, repairs to the farm buildings.

    Although he was married, with children, his was a solitary disposition; he liked best to work alone. It pleased him when he was given a bank to
10 build up, or a gate to mend at the far end of the peninsula, where the sea surrounded the farm land on either side. Then, at midday, he would pause and eat the pasty that his wife had baked for him, and sitting on the cliff's edge would watch the birds. Autumn was best for this, better than spring. In spring the birds flew inland, purposeful, intent; they knew where they were
15 bound, the rhythm and ritual of their life brooked no delay. In autumn those that had not migrated overseas but remained to pass the winter were caught up in the same driving urge, but because migration was denied them followed a pattern of their own. Great flocks of them came to the peninsula, restless, uneasy, spending themselves in motion; now wheeling, circling in
20 the sky, now settling to feed on the rich new-turned soil, but even when they fed it was as though they did so without hunger, without desire. Restlessness drove them to the skies again.

    Black and white, jackdaw and gull, mingled in strange partnership, seeking some sort of liberation, never satisfied, never still. Flocks of star-
25 lings, rustling like silk, flew to fresh pasture, driven by the same necessity of movement, and the smaller birds, the finches and the larks, scattered from tree to hedge as if compelled.

    Nat watched them, and he watched the sea-birds too. Down in the bay they waited for the tide. They had more patience. Oyster-catchers, redshank,
30 sanderling, and curlew watched by the water's edge; as the slow sea sucked at the shore and then withdrew, leaving the strip of seaweed bare and the shingle churned, the sea-birds raced and ran upon the beaches. Then that same impulse to flight seized upon them too. Crying, whistling, calling, they skimmed the placid sea and left the shore. Make haste, make speed, hurry
35 and be gone: yet where, and to what purpose? The restless urge of autumn,

2 *mellow:* gentle and mild

2 *linger:* stay longer than expected

3 *hedgerow:* Hecke

7 *hedging:* looking after the hedges/hedgerows

7 *thatching:* repairing thatched roofs (= Reetdächer)

9 *bank:* (Erd-)Wall, Böschung

10 *peninsula:* Halbinsel

14 *intent (adj):* concentrated

15 *be bound (for):* unterwegs sein nach

15 *brook sth. (fml):* tolerate, accept sth.

17 *driving urge:* (an-) treibender Drang

17 *deny sb. sth.:* jdm. etwas vorenthalten

19 *spend oneself:* sich verausgaben

19 *wheel (v):* fly in a circle

23 *jackdaw:* Dohle

23 *gull:* Möwe

24 *starling:* Star (Vogel)

26 *finch:* Fink

26 *lark:* Lerche

31 *shore:* coast

31 *seaweed:* Tang

32 *shingle:* Geröll

32 *churn sth.:* etwas aufwühlen

33 *seize upon sb.* [si:z] *(fml):* von jdm. Besitz ergreifen

34 *placid:* calm

unsatisfying, sad, had put a spell upon them and they must flock, and wheel, and cry; they must spill themselves of motion before winter came.

Perhaps, thought Nat, munching his pasty by the cliff's edge, a message comes to the birds in autumn, like a warning. Winter is coming. Many of
5 them perish. And like people who, apprehensive of death before their time, drive themselves to work or folly, the birds do likewise.

The birds had been more restless than ever this fall of the year, the agitation more marked because the days were still. As the tractor traced its path up and down the western hills, the figure of the farmer silhouetted on the
10 driving-seat, the whole machine and the man upon it would be lost momentarily in the great cloud of wheeling, crying birds. There were many more than usual, Nat was sure of this. Always, in autumn, they followed the plough, but not in great flocks like these, nor with such clamour.

Nat remarked upon it, when hedging was finished for the day. 'Yes,' said
15 the farmer, 'there are more birds about than usual; I've noticed it too. And daring, some of them, taking no notice of the tractor. One or two gulls came so close to my head this afternoon I thought they'd knock my cap off! As it was, I could scarcely see what I was doing, when they were overhead and I had the sun in my eyes. I have a notion the weather will change. It will be a
20 hard winter. That's why the birds are restless.'

Nat, tramping home across the fields and down the lane to his cottage, saw the birds still flocking over the western hills, in the last glow of the sun. No wind, and the grey sea calm and full. Campion in bloom yet in the hedges, and the air mild. The farmer was right, though, and it was that night the
25 weather turned. Nat's bedroom faced east. He woke just after two and heard the wind in the chimney. Not the storm and bluster of a sou'westerly gale, bringing the rain, but east wind, cold and dry. It sounded hollow in the chimney, and a loose slate rattled on the roof. Nat listened, and he could hear the sea roaring in the bay. Even the air in the small bedroom had turned
30 chill: a draught came under the skirting of the door, blowing upon the bed. Nat drew the blanket round him, leant closer to the back of his sleeping wife, and stayed wakeful, watchful, aware of misgiving without cause.

Then he heard the tapping on the window. There was no creeper on the cottage walls to break loose and scratch upon the pane. He listened, and the
35 tapping continued until, irritated by the sound, Nat got out of bed and went to the window. He opened it, and as he did so something brushed his hand, jabbing at his knuckles, grazing the skin. Then he saw the flutter of the wings and it was gone, over the roof, behind the cottage.

It was a bird, what kind of bird he could not tell. The wind must have
40 driven it to shelter on the sill.

He shut the window and went back to bed, but feeling his knuckles wet put his mouth to the scratch. The bird had drawn blood. Frightened, he supposed, and bewildered, the bird, seeking shelter, had stabbed at him in the darkness. Once more he settled himself to sleep.
45 Presently the tapping came again, this time more forceful, more insistent, and now his wife woke at the sound, and turning in the bed said to him, 'See to the window, Nat, it's rattling.'

---

1 *flock (v):* in Scharen zusammenkommen

2 *spill oneself of sth.:* sich von etwas befreien

5 *perish:* die

5 *be apprehensive of sth. (fml):* be afraid of sth.

6 *folly:* foolish behaviour

7 *fall (AE):* autumn

7 *agitation:* restless excitement

8 *marked:* auffällig

13 *clamour:* sound of many voices

16 *daring (adj):* brave, willing to take risks

23 *be in bloom:* blühen

26 *chimney:* Schornstein

26 *bluster (n):* wind

26 *gale:* severe storm

30 *chill (adj):* cold

30 *draught* [drɑːft]: Luftzug

32 *misgiving (n):* feeling that sth. is wrong

33 *creeper:* Kletterpflanze

37 *jab:* stechen

37 *knuckle* ['nʌkl]: Fingerknöchel

40 *sill:* Fensterbrett, Sims

42 *scratch:* Kratzer

43 *bewildered:* confused

43 *stab at sb.:* attack sb. with a sharp object

45 *presently:* soon afterwards

47 *rattle:* make a sound as if loose

'I've already seen to it,' he told her, 'there's some bird there, trying to get in. Can't you hear the wind? It's blowing from the east, driving the birds to shelter.'

'Send them away,' she said, 'I can't sleep with that noise.'

5 He went to the window for the second time, and now when he opened it there was not one bird upon the sill but half a dozen; they flew straight into his face, attacking him.

He shouted, striking out at them with his arms, scattering them; like the first one, they flew over the roof and disappeared. Quickly he let the window 10 fall and latched it.

'Did you hear that?' he said. 'They went for me. Tried to peck my eyes.' He stood by the window, peering into the darkness, and could see nothing. His wife, heavy with sleep, murmured from the bed.

'I'm not making it up,' he said, angry at her suggestion. 'I tell you the birds 15 were on the sill, trying to get into the room.'

Suddenly a frightened cry came from the room across the passage where the children slept.

'It's Jill,' said his wife, roused at the sound, sitting up in bed. 'Go to her, see what's the matter.'

20 Nat lit the candle, but when he opened the bedroom door to cross the passage the draught blew out the flame.

There came a second cry of terror, this time from both children, and stumbling into their room he felt the beating of wings about him in the darkness. The window was wide open. Through it came the birds, hitting first the 25 ceiling and the walls, then swerving in mid-flight, turning to the children in their beds.

'It's all right, I'm here,' shouted Nat, and the children flung themselves, screaming, upon him, while in the darkness the birds rose and dived and came for him again.

30 'What is it, Nat, what's happened?' his wife called from the further bedroom, and swiftly he pushed the children through the door to the passage and shut it upon them, so that he was alone now, in their bedroom, with the birds.

He seized a blanket from the nearest bed, and using it as a weapon flung 35 it to right and left about him in the air. He felt the thud of bodies, heard the fluttering of wings, but they were not yet defeated, for again and again they returned to the assault, jabbing his hands, his head, the little stabbing beaks sharp as a pointed fork. The blanket became a weapon of defence; he wound it about his head, and then in greater darkness beat at the birds with his 40 bare hands. He dared not stumble to the door and open it, lest in doing so the birds should follow him.

How long he fought with them in the darkness he could not tell, but at last the beating of the wings about him lessened and then withdrew, and through the density of the blanket he was aware of light. He waited, listened; 45 there was no sound except the fretful crying of one of the children from the bedroom beyond. The fluttering, the whirring of the wings had ceased.

8 *scatter sth.:* etwas zerstreuen

10 *latch sth.:* fasten sth. with a latch (= Riegel)

12 *peer (v):* look

16 *passage:* corridor

18 *rouse sb.:* make sb. become active

23 *stumble:* stolpern

25 *swerve:* move in a sharp curve

34 *weapon* ['wepən]: Waffe

35 *thud (n):* Aufprall

36 *defeat sb.:* jdn. besiegen

37 *assault (n):* attack

37 *beak:* Schnabel

40 *lest:* damit nicht

44 *density:* thickness

45 *fretful:* worried, upset

46 *whirring:* Surren

He took the blanket from his head and stared about him. The cold grey morning light exposed the room. Dawn, and the open window, had called the living birds; the dead lay on the floor. Nat gazed at the little corpses, shocked and horrified. They were all small birds, none of any size; there
5 must have been fifty of them lying there upon the floor. There were robins, finches, sparrows, blue tits, larks and bramblings, birds that by nature's law kept to their own flock and their own territory, and now, joining one with another in their urge for battle, had destroyed themselves against the bedroom walls, or in the strife had been destroyed by him. Some had lost
10 feathers in the fight, others had blood, his blood, upon their beaks.

Sickened, Nat went to the window and stared out across his patch of garden to the fields.

It was bitter cold, and the ground had all the hard black look of frost. Not white frost, to shine in the morning sun, but the black frost that the east
15 wind brings. The sea, fiercer now with the turning tide, white-capped and steep, broke harshly in the bay. Of the birds there was no sign. Not a sparrow chattered in the hedge beyond the garden gate, no early missel-thrush or blackbird pecked on the grass for worms. There was no sound at all but the east wind and the sea.
20 Nat shut the window and the door of the small bedroom, and went back across the passage to his own. His wife sat up in bed, one child asleep beside her, the smaller in her arms, his face bandaged. The curtains were tightly drawn across the window, the candles lit. Her face looked garish in the yellow light. She shook her head for silence.
25 'He's sleeping now,' she whispered, 'but only just. Something must have cut him, there was blood at the corner of his eyes. Jill said it was the birds. She said she woke up, and the birds were in the room.'

His wife looked up at Nat, searching his face for confirmation. She looked terrified, bewildered, and he did not want her to know that he was also
30 shaken, dazed almost, by the events of the past few hours.

'There are birds in there,' he said, 'dead birds, nearly fifty of them. Robins, wrens, all the little birds from hereabouts. It's as though a madness seized them, with the east wind.' He sat down on the bed beside his wife, and held her hand. 'It's the weather,' he said, 'it must be that, it's the hard weather.
35 They aren't the birds, maybe, from here around. They've been driven down, from up country.'

'But Nat,' whispered his wife, 'it's only this night that the weather turned. There's been no snow to drive them. And they can't be hungry yet. There's food for them, out there, in the fields.'
40 'It's the weather,' repeated Nat. 'I tell you, it's the weather.'

His face too was drawn and tired, like hers. They stared at one another for a while without speaking.

'I'll go downstairs and make a cup of tea,' he said.

The sight of the kitchen reassured him. The cups and saucers, neatly
45 stacked upon the dresser, the table and chairs, his wife's roll of knitting on her basket chair, the children's toys in a corner cupboard.

2 *expose sth.:* make sth. visible

2 *dawn (n):* first light of morning

3 *gaze (v):* stare

3 *corpse:* dead body

5 *robin:* Rotkehlchen

6 *sparrow:* Sperling

6 *blue tit:* Blaumeise

6 *brambling:* Bergfink

9 *strife:* fight, battle

15 *fierce:* grimmig

15 *white-capped:* mit Schaumkronen

16 *steep:* steil

17 *missel-thrush:* = mistle thrush (= Misteldrossel)

18 *blackbird:* Amsel

23 *garish:* grell

30 *shaken:* erschüttert

30 *dazed:* benommen

32 *wren* [ren]: Zaunkönig

41 *drawn:* angespannt

44 *reassure sb.* [ˌriːəˈʃʊə(r)]: make sb. feel secure

45 *dresser:* Kommode

45 *roll of knitting* [ˈnɪtɪŋ]: Strickzeug

He knelt down, raked out the old embers and relit the fire. The glowing sticks brought normality, the steaming kettle and the brown teapot comfort and security. He drank his tea, carried a cup up to his wife. Then he washed in the scullery, and, putting on his boots, opened the back door.

5   The sky was hard and leaden, and the brown hills that had gleamed in the sun the day before looked dark and bare. The east wind, like a razor, stripped the trees, and the leaves, crackling and dry, shivered and scattered with the wind's blast. Nat stubbed the earth with his boot. It was frozen hard. He had never known a change so swift and sudden. Black winter had
10   descended in a single night.

The children were awake now. Jill was chattering upstairs and young Johnny crying once again. Nat heard his wife's voice, soothing, comforting. Presently they came down. He had breakfast ready for them, and the routine of the day began.

15   'Did you drive away the birds?' asked Jill, restored to calm because of the kitchen fire, because of day, because of breakfast.

'Yes, they've all gone now,' said Nat. 'It was the east wind brought them in. They were frightened and lost, they wanted shelter.'

'They tried to peck us,' said Jill. 'They went for Johnny's eyes.'

20   'Fright made them do that,' said Nat. 'They didn't know where they were, in the dark bedroom.'

'I hope they won't come again,' said Jill. 'Perhaps if we put bread for them outside the window they will eat that and fly away.'

She finished her breakfast and then went for her coat and hood, her
25   school books and her satchel. Nat said nothing, but his wife looked at him across the table. A silent message passed between them.

'I'll walk with her to the bus,' he said, 'I don't go to the farm today.'

And while the child was washing in the scullery he said to his wife, 'Keep all the windows closed, and the doors too. Just to be on the safe side. I'll go
30   to the farm. Find out if they heard anything in the night.' Then he walked with his small daughter up the lane. She seemed to have forgotten her experience of the night before. She danced ahead of him, chasing the leaves, her face whipped with the cold and rosy under the pixie hood.

'Is it going to snow, Dad?' she said. 'It's cold enough.'

35   He glanced up at the bleak sky, felt the wind tear at his shoulders.

'No,' he said, 'it's not going to snow. This is a black winter, not a white one.'

All the while he searched the hedgerows for the birds, glanced over the top of them to the fields beyond, looked to the small wood above the farm where the rooks and jackdaws gathered. He saw none.

40   The other children waited by the bus-stop, muffled, hooded like Jill, the faces white and pinched with cold.

Jill ran to them, waving. 'My Dad says it won't snow,' she called, 'it's going to be a black winter.'

She said nothing of the birds. She began to push and struggle with
45   another little girl. The bus came ambling up the hill. Nat saw her on to it, then turned and walked back towards the farm. It was not his day for work,

1 *rake sth. out:* etwas herauskehren

1 *embers:* hot ashes

2 *comfort:* Trost

4 *scullery:* small room for washing

5 *leaden* ['lɛdn]: bleiern

6 *bare:* kahl

6 *razor:* Rasiermesser

7 *crackle:* make a dry sound

7 *shiver:* shake from the cold

8 *blast (n):* strong wind

9 *swift:* fast

10 *descend* [dɪ'send]: herabsteigen

12 *soothe sb./sth.* [suːð] : make sb./sth. feel less pain

15 *restore sb. (to sth.):* put sb. back in their former state

25 *satchel:* school bag

31 *lane:* country road

33 *whip sth.:* etwas peitschen

33 *pixie (adj):* fairy-like

35 *bleak:* trostlos

39 *rook:* Saatkrähe

40 *muffled:* vermummt

41 *pinched:* verkniffen

44 *struggle (v):* fight

45 *amble:* move slowly

45 *saw her on to it* = waited until she was on the bus

but he wanted to satisfy himself that all was well. Jim, the cowman, was clat-
tering in the yard.

'Boss around?' asked Nat.

'Gone to market,' said Jim. 'It's Tuesday, isn't it?'

5 He clumped off round the corner of a shed. He had no time for Nat. Nat
was said to be superior. Read books, and the like. Nat had forgotten it was
Tuesday. This showed how the events of the preceding night had shaken
him. He went to the back door of the farm-house and heard Mrs Trigg
singing in the kitchen, the wireless making a background to her song.

10 'Are you there, missus?' called out Nat.

She came to the door, beaming, broad, a good-tempered woman.

'Hullo, Mr Hocken,' she said. 'Can you tell me where this cold is coming
from? Is it Russia? I've never seen such a change. And it's going on, the wireless says. Something to do with the Arctic circle.'

15 'We didn't turn on the wireless this morning,' said Nat. 'Fact is, we had
trouble in the night.'

'Kiddies poorly?'

'No ...' He hardly knew how to explain it. Now, in daylight, the battle of the
birds would sound absurd.

20 He tried to tell Mrs Trigg what had happened, but he could see from her
eyes that she thought his story was the result of a nightmare.

'Sure they were real birds,' she said, smiling, 'with proper feathers and all?
Not the funny-shaped kind, that the men see after closing hours on a
Saturday night?'

25 'Mrs Trigg,' he said, 'there are fifty dead birds, robins, wrens, and such,
lying low on the floor of the children's bedroom. They went for me; they tried
to go for young Johnny's eyes.'

Mrs Trigg stared at him doubtfully.

'Well there, now,' she answered, 'I suppose the weather brought them.
30 Once in the bedroom, they wouldn't know where they were to. Foreign birds
maybe, from that Arctic circle.'

'No,' said Nat, 'they were the birds you see about here every day.'

'Funny thing,' said Mrs Trigg, 'no explaining it, really. You ought to write
up and ask the Guardian. They'd have some answer for it. Well, I must be
35 getting on.'

She nodded, smiled, and went back into the kitchen.

Nat, dissatisfied, turned to the farm-gate. Had it not been for those
corpses on the bedroom floor, which he must now collect and bury some-
where, he would have considered the tale exaggeration too.

40 Jim was standing by the gate.

'Had any trouble with the birds?' asked Nat.

'Birds? What birds?'

'We got them up our place last night. Scores of them, came in the children's bedroom. Quite savage they were.'

45 'Oh?' It took time for anything to penetrate Jim's head. 'Never heard of
birds acting savage,' he said at length. 'They get tame, like, sometimes. I've
seen them come to the windows for crumbs.'

---

1 *clatter (v):* work noisily

5 *clump off:* walk away heavily

6 *superior:* überheblich, eingebildet

9 *wireless (BE, old-fashioned):* radio

10 *missus:* informal form of address for a married woman

11 *beam (v):* smile

11 *good-tempered:* friendly, easy-going

17 *Kiddies poorly?:* Are the children ill?

26 *low:* dead

34 *the Guardian:* British newspaper

43 *score:* large number

44 *savage (adj):* wild, aggressive

46 *at length:* after a while

46 *tame (adj):* zahm

47 *crumb* [krʌm]: small bit of bread

'These birds last night weren't tame.'

'No? Cold maybe. Hungry. You put out some crumbs.'

Jim was no more interested than Mrs Trigg had been. It was, Nat thought, like air-raids in the war. No one down this end of the country knew what the
5 Plymouth folk had seen and suffered. You had to endure something yourself before it touched you.

He walked back along the lane and crossed the stile to his cottage. He found his wife in the kitchen with young Johnny.

'See anyone?' she asked.

10 'Mrs Trigg and Jim,' he answered. 'I don't think they believed me. Anyway, nothing wrong up there.'

'You might take the birds away,' she said. 'I daren't go into the room to make the beds until you do. I'm scared.'

'Nothing to scare you now,' said Nat. 'They're dead, aren't they?'

15 He went up with a sack and dropped the stiff bodies into it, one by one. Yes, there were fifty of them, all told. Just the ordinary common birds of the hedgerow, nothing as large even as a thrush. It must have been fright that made them act the way they did. Blue tits, wrens, it was incredible to think of the power of their small beaks, jabbing at his face and hands the night
20 before. He took the sack out into the garden and was faced now with a fresh problem. The ground was too hard to dig. It was frozen solid, yet no snow had fallen, nothing had happened in the past hours but the coming of the east wind. It was unnatural, queer. The weather prophets must be right. The change was something connected with the Arctic circle.

25 The wind seemed to cut him to the bone as he stood there, uncertainly, holding the sack. He could see the white-capped seas breaking down under in the bay. He decided to take the birds to the shore and bury them.

When he reached the beach below the headland he could scarcely stand, the force of the east wind was so strong. It hurt to draw breath, and his bare
30 hands were blue. Never had he known such cold, not in all the bad winters he could remember. It was low tide. He crunched his way over the shingle to the softer sand and then, his back to the wind, ground a pit in the sand with his heel. He meant to drop the birds into it, but as he opened up the sack the force of the wind carried them, lifted them, as though in flight again, and
35 they were blown away from him along the beach, tossed like feathers, spread and scattered, the bodies of the fifty frozen birds. There was something ugly in the sight. He did not like it. The dead birds were swept away from him by the wind.

'The tide will take them when it turns,' he said to himself.

40 He looked out to sea and watched the crested breakers, combing green. They rose stiffly, curled, and broke again, and because it was ebb tide the roar was distant, more remote, lacking the sound and thunder of the flood.

Then he saw them. The gulls. Out there, riding the seas.

What he had thought at first to be the white caps of the waves were gulls.
45 Hundreds, thousands, tens of thousands ... They rose and fell in the trough of the seas, heads to the wind, like a mighty fleet at anchor, waiting on the tide. To eastward, and to the west, the gulls were there. They stretched as far

---

4 *air-raid:* Luftangriffe

5 *endure sth.:* etwas ertragen

7 *stile:* steps for crossing over a fence between fields

23 *queer:* strange

28 *headland:* high land extending into the sea

31 *low tide:* Ebbe

31 *crunch:* make a crunching sound (= Knirschen) while walking

32 *pit:* small hole

35 *toss sth.:* throw sth.

40 *crested:* capped with foam

40 *breaker:* wave that collapses as it reaches the shore

40 *comb (v):* move steadily

45 *trough* [trɒf]: Wellental

46 *mighty:* powerful

46 *fleet:* Flotte

as his eye could reach, in close formation, line upon line. Had the sea been
still they would have covered the bay like a white cloud, head to head, body
packed to body. Only the east wind, whipping the sea to breakers, hid them
from the shore.

5   Nat turned, and leaving the beach climbed the steep path home.
Someone should know of this. Someone should be told. Something was
happening, because of the east wind and the weather, that he did not understand. He wondered if he should go to the call-box by the bus-stop and ring
up the police. Yet what could they do? What could anyone do? Tens and
10 thousands of gulls riding the sea there, in the bay, because of storm, because
of hunger. The police would think him mad, or drunk, or take the statement
from him with great calm. 'Thank you. Yes, the matter has already been
reported. The hard weather is driving the birds inland in great numbers.' Nat
looked about him. Still no sign of any other bird. Perhaps the cold had sent
15 them all from up country? As he drew near to the cottage his wife came to
meet him, at the door. She called to him, excited. 'Nat,' she said, 'it's on the
wireless. They've just read out a special news bulletin. I've written it down.'

'What's on the wireless?' he said.

'About the birds,' she said. 'It's not only here, it's everywhere. In London,
20 all over the country. Something has happened to the birds.'

Together they went into the kitchen. He read the piece of paper lying on
the table.

'Statement from the Home Office at eleven a.m. today. Reports from all
over the country are coming in hourly about the vast quantity of birds
25 flocking above towns, villages, and outlying districts, causing obstruction
and damage and even attacking individuals. It is thought that the Arctic air
stream, at present covering the British Isles, is causing birds to migrate
south in immense numbers, and that intense hunger may drive these birds
to attack human beings. Householders are warned to see to their windows,
30 doors, and chimneys, and to take reasonable precautions for the safety of
their children. A further statement will be issued later.' A kind of excitement
seized Nat; he looked at his wife in triumph.

'There you are,' he said, 'let's hope they'll hear that at the farm. Mrs Trigg
will know it wasn't any story. It's true. All over the country. I've been telling
35 myself all morning there's something wrong. And just now, down on the
beach, I looked out to sea and there are gulls, thousands of them, tens of
thousands, you couldn't put a pin between their heads, and they're all out
there, riding on the sea, waiting.'

'What are they waiting for, Nat?' she asked.
40   He stared at her, then looked down again at the piece of paper. 'I don't
know,' he said slowly. 'It says here the birds are hungry.' He went over to the
drawer where he kept his hammer and tools.

'What are you going to do, Nat?'

'See to the windows and the chimneys too, like they tell you.'
45   'You think they would break in, with the windows shut? Those sparrows
and robins and such? Why, how could they?'

24 *vast:* huge

25 *obstruction:* Behinderung

30 *precaution:*
Vorsichtsmaßnahme

31 *issue a statement:* eine
Erklärung herausgeben

42 *drawer* [drɔː(r)]: Schublade

He did not answer. He was not thinking of the robins and the sparrows. He was thinking of the gulls ...

He went upstairs and worked there the rest of the morning, boarding the windows of the bedrooms, filling up the chimney bases. Good job it was his
5 free day and he was not working at the farm. It reminded him of the old days, at the beginning of the war. He was not married then, and he had made all the blackout boards for his mother's house in Plymouth. Made the shelter too. Not that it had been of any use, when the moment came. He wondered if they would take these precautions up at the farm. He doubted
10 it. Too easy-going, Harry Trigg and his missus. Maybe they'd laugh at the whole thing. Go off to a dance or a whist drive.

'Dinner's ready.' She called him, from the kitchen.

'All right. Coming down.'

He was pleased with his handiwork. The frames fitted nicely over the
15 little panes and at the base of the chimneys.

When dinner was over and his wife was washing up, Nat switched on the one o'clock news. The same announcement was repeated, the one which she had taken down during the morning, but the news bulletin enlarged upon it. 'The flocks of birds have caused dislocation in all areas,' read the
20 announcer, 'and in London the sky was so dense at ten o'clock this morning that it seemed as if the city was covered by a vast black cloud.

'The birds settled on roof-tops, on window ledges and on chimneys. The species included blackbird, thrush, the common house-sparrow, and, as might be expected in the metropolis, a vast quantity of pigeons and star-
25 lings, and that frequenter of the London river, the black-headed gull. The sight has been so unusual that traffic came to a standstill in many thorough-fares, work was abandoned in shops and offices, and the streets and pave-ments were crowded with people standing about to watch the birds.'

Various incidents were recounted, the suspected reason of cold and
30 hunger stated again, and warnings to householders repeated. The announc-er's voice was smooth and suave. Nat had the impression that this man, in particular, treated the whole business as he would an elaborate joke. There would be others like him, hundreds of them, who did not know what it was to struggle in darkness with a flock of birds. There would be parties tonight
35 in London, like the ones they gave on election nights. People standing about, shouting and laughing, getting drunk. 'Come and watch the birds!'

Nat switched off the wireless. He got up and started work on the kitchen windows. His wife watched him, young Johnny at her heels.

'What, boards for down here too?' she said. 'Why, I'll have to light up
40 before three o'clock. I see no call for boards down here.'

'Better be sure than sorry,' answered Nat. 'I'm not going to take any chances.'

'What they ought to do,' she said, 'is to call the army out and shoot the birds. That would soon scare them off.'

45 'Let them try,' said Nat. 'How'd they set about it?'

'They have the army to the docks,' she answered, 'when the dockers strike. The soldiers go down and unload the ships.'

3 *board sth. (v):* cover sth. with boards

4 *base:* Sockel

4 *good job (infml):* luckily

7 *blackout boards:* during WW II windows had to be made dark during air raids

8 *shelter:* Schutzraum

11 *whist drive (BE):* social event at which whist (a card game) is played

18 *enlarge upon sth.:* add information to sth.

19 *dislocation:* disturbance

20 *dense:* bedeckt

24 *pigeon:* Taube

25 *frequenter:* common visitor

25 *black-headed gull:* Lachmöwe

26 *thoroughfare:* major road

27 *abandon sth.:* leave sth. undone

29 *recount sth.:* report sth.

31 *suave:* confident and elegant

32 *elaborate:* large and complex

40 *call (n):* (here) reason

45 *How'd they set about it?* = What exactly would they do?

'Yes,' said Nat, 'and the population of London is eight million or more. Think of all the buildings, all the flats, and houses. Do you think they've enough soldiers to go round shooting birds from every roof?'

'I don't know. But something should be done. They ought to do
5 something.'

Nat thought to himself that 'they' were no doubt considering the problem at that very moment, but whatever 'they' decided to do in London and the big cities would not help the people here, three hundred miles away. Each householder must look after his own.

10 'How are we off for food?' he said.

'Now, Nat, whatever next?'

'Never mind. What have you got in the larder?'

'It's shopping day tomorrow, you know that. I don't keep uncooked food hanging about, it goes off. Butcher doesn't call till the day after. But I can
15 bring back something when I go in tomorrow.'

Nat did not want to scare her. He thought it possible that she might not go to town tomorrow. He looked in the larder for himself, and in the cupboard where she kept her tins. They would do, for a couple of days. Bread was low.

20 'What about the baker?'

'He comes tomorrow too.'

He saw she had flour. If the baker did not call she had enough to bake one loaf.

'We'd be better off in the old days,' he said, 'when the women baked twice
25 a week, and had pilchards salted, and there was food for a family to last a siege, if need be.'

'I've tried the children with tinned fish, they don't like it,' she said.

Nat went on hammering the boards across the kitchen windows. Candles. They were low in candles too. That must be another thing she
30 meant to buy tomorrow. Well, it could not be helped. They must go early to bed tonight. That was, if …

He got up and went out of the back door and stood in the garden, looking down towards the sea. There had been no sun all day, and now, at barely three o'clock, a kind of darkness had already come, the sky sullen, heavy,
35 colourless like salt. He could hear the vicious sea drumming on the rocks. He walked down the path, half-way to the beach. And then he stopped. He could see the tide had turned. The rock that had shown in mid-morning was now covered, but it was not the sea that held his eyes. The gulls had risen. They were circling, hundreds of them, thousands of them, lifting their wings
40 against the wind. It was the gulls that made the darkening of the sky. And they were silent. They made not a sound. They just went on soaring and circling, rising, falling, trying their strength against the wind.

Nat turned. He ran up the path, back to the cottage.

'I'm going for Jill,' he said. 'I'll wait for her, at the bus-stop.'
45 'What's the matter?' asked his wife. 'You've gone quite white.'

'Keep Johnny inside,' he said. 'Keep the door shut. Light up now, and draw the curtains.'

10 *How are we off for food?* = How much food have got?

11 *Whatever next?* = What's the next problem you're going to discover?

12 *larder:* cupboard or small room where food is kept

14 *go off (infml):* spoil, turn bad

14 *butcher:* person who sells meat

14 *call (v):* visit

23 *loaf:* Brotlaib

25 *pilchard:* sardine

26 *siege:* Belagerung

34 *sullen:* düster

35 *vicious* ['vɪʃəs]: bösartig

41 *soar:* (in der Luft) segeln

42 *try sth.:* test sth.

'It's only just gone three,' she said.

'Never mind. Do what I tell you.'

He looked inside the toolshed, outside the back door. Nothing there of much use. A spade was too heavy, and a fork no good. He took the hoe. It
5   was the only possible tool, and light enough to carry.

He started walking up the lane to the bus-stop, and now and again glanced back over his shoulder.

The gulls had risen higher now, their circles were broader, wider, they were spreading out in huge formation across the sky.

10   He hurried on; although he knew the bus would not come to the top of the hill before four o'clock he had to hurry. He passed no one on the way. He was glad of this. No time to stop and chatter.

At the top of the hill he waited. He was much too soon. There was half an hour still to go. The east wind came whipping across the fields from the
15   higher ground. He stamped his feet and blew upon his hands. In the distance he could see the clay hills, white and clean, against the heavy pallor of the sky. Something black rose from behind them, like a smudge at first, then widening, becoming deeper, and the smudge became a cloud, and the cloud divided again into five other clouds, spreading north, east, south and west,
20   and they were not clouds at all; they were birds. He watched them travel across the sky, and as one section passed overhead, within two or three hundred feet of him, he knew from their speed, they were bound inland, up country, they had no business with the people here on the peninsula. They were rooks, crows, jackdaws, magpies, jays, all birds that usually preyed
25   upon the smaller species; but this afternoon they were bound on some other mission.

'They've been given the towns,' thought Nat, 'they know what they have to do. We don't matter so much here. The gulls will serve for us. The others go to the towns.'

30   He went to the call-box, stepped inside and lifted the receiver. The exchange would do. They would pass the message on.

'I'm speaking from Highway,' he said, 'by the bus-stop. I want to report large formations of birds travelling up country. The gulls are also forming in the bay.'

35   'All right,' answered the voice, laconic, weary.

'You'll be sure and pass this message on to the proper quarter?'

'Yes ... yes ...' Impatient now, fed-up. The buzzing note resumed.

'She's another,' thought Nat, 'she doesn't care. Maybe she's had to answer calls all day. She hopes to go to the pictures tonight. She'll squeeze some
40   fellow's hand, and point up at the sky, and say "Look at all them birds!" She doesn't care.'

The bus came lumbering up the hill. Jill climbed out and three or four other children. The bus went on towards the town. 'What's the hoe for, Dad?'

45   They crowded around him, laughing, pointing.

4 *spade:* Spaten
4 *fork:* Gabel(-spaten)
4 *hoe:* Hacke
16 *clay hill:* Lehmhügel
16 *pallor:* Blässe
17 *smudge:* Schmutzfleck
24 *magpie:* Elster
24 *jay:* Eichelhäher
24 *prey upon sth.:* auf etwas Beute machen
28 *serve for sth.:* be good enough for sth.
30 *receiver:* Hörer
31 *exchange:* Vermittlung
35 *laconic:* kurz angebunden
35 *weary:* very tired
36 *quarter:* address
37 *impatient:* ungeduldig
37 *fed-up (infml):* completely disinterested
37 *resume:* start again
39 *pictures:* cinema
39 *squeeze sth.:* etwas drücken
40 *fellow (infml):* Kerl
42 *lumber (v):* move slowly and heavily
45 *crowd (v):* form a crowd

'I just brought it along,' he said. 'Come on now, let's get home. It's cold, no hanging about. Here, you. I'll watch you across the fields, see how fast you can run.'

He was speaking to Jill's companions who came from different families, living in the council houses. A short cut would take them to the cottages.

'We want to play a bit in the lane,' said one of them.

'No, you don't. You go off home, or I'll tell your mammy.' They whispered to one another, round-eyed, then scuttled off across the fields. Jill stared at her father, her mouth sullen.

'We always play in the lane,' she said.

'Not tonight, you don't,' he said. 'Come on now, no dawdling.' He could see the gulls now, circling the fields, coming in towards the land. Still silent. Still no sound.

'Look, Dad, look over there, look at all the gulls.'

'Yes. Hurry, now.'

'Where are they flying to? Where are they going?'

'Up country, I dare say. Where it's warmer.'

He seized her hand and dragged her after him along the lane.

'Don't go so fast. I can't keep up.'

The gulls were copying the rooks and crows. They were spreading out in formation across the sky. They headed, in bands of thousands, to the four compass points.

'Dad, what is it? What are the gulls doing?'

They were not intent upon their flight, as the crows, as the jackdaws had been. They still circled overhead. Nor did they fly so high. It was as though they waited upon some signal. As though some decision had yet to be given. The order was not clear.

'Do you want me to carry you, Jill? Here, come pick-a-back.' This way he might put on speed; but he was wrong. Jill was heavy. She kept slipping. And she was crying too. His sense of urgency, of fear, had communicated itself to the child.

'I wish the gulls would go away. I don't like them. They're coming closer to the lane.'

He put her down again. He started running, swinging Jill after him. As they went past the farm turning he saw the farmer backing his car out of the garage. Nat called to him.

'Can you give us a lift?' he said.

'What's that?'

Mr Trigg turned in the driving seat and stared at them. Then a smile came to his cheerful, rubicund face.

'It looks as though we're in for some fun,' he said. 'Have you seen the gulls? Jim and I are going to take a crack at them. Everyone's gone bird crazy, talking of nothing else. I hear you were troubled in the night. Want a gun?'

Nat shook his head.

The small car was packed. There was just room for Jill, if she crouched on top of petrol tins on the back seat.

4 *companion:* Begleiter
5 *council house:* Sozialwohnung
5 *short cut:* Abkürzung
8 *scuttle off:* run off
11 *dawdle:* trödeln
17 *I dare say (BE):* I think
20 *crow:* Krähe
28 *pick-a-back:* huckepack
30 *urgency:* Dringlichkeit
35 *farm turning:* road leading to the farm
37 *lift (n):* ride
40 *rubicund:* reddish
42 *take a crack at sth.:* try shooting sth.
45 *crouch:* hocken

'I don't want a gun,' said Nat, 'but I'd be obliged if you'd run Jill home. She's scared of the birds.'

He spoke briefly. He did not want to talk in front of Jill. 'OK,' said the farmer, 'I'll take her home. Why don't you stop behind and join the shooting
5 match? We'll make the feathers fly.' Jill climbed in, and turning the car the driver sped up the lane. Nat followed after. Trigg must be crazy. What use was a gun against a sky of birds?

Now Nat was not responsible for Jill he had time to look about him. The birds were circling still, above the fields. Mostly herring gull, but the black-
10 backed gull amongst them. Usually they kept apart. Now they were united. Some bond had brought them together. It was the black-backed gull that attacked the smaller birds, and even new-born lambs, so he'd heard. He'd never seen it done. He remembered this now, though, looking above him in the sky. They were coming in towards the farm. They were circling lower in
15 the sky, and the black-backed gulls were to the front, the black-backed gulls were leading. The farm, then, was their target. They were making for the farm.

Nat increased his pace towards his own cottage. He saw the farmer's car turn and come back along the lane. It drew up beside him with a jerk.
20 'The kid has run inside,' said the farmer. 'Your wife was watching for her. Well, what do you make of it? They're saying in town the Russians have done it. The Russians have poisoned the birds.'

'How could they do that?' asked Nat.

'Don't ask me. You know how stories get around. Will you join my
25 shooting match?'

'No, I'll get along home. The wife will be worried else.'

'My missus says if you could eat gull, there'd be some sense in it,' said Trigg, 'we'd have roast gull, baked gull, and pickle 'em into the bargain. You wait until I let off a few barrels into the brutes. That'll scare 'em.'
30 'Have you boarded your windows?' asked Nat.

'No. Lot of nonsense. They like to scare you on the wireless. I've had more to do today than to go round boarding up my windows.'

'I'd board them now, if I were you.'

'Garn. You're windy. Like to come to our place to sleep?'
35 'No, thanks all the same.'

'All right. See you in the morning. Give you a gull breakfast.' The farmer grinned and turned his car to the farm entrance. Nat hurried on. Past the little wood, past the old barn, and then across the stile to the remaining field.
40 As he jumped the stile he heard the whirr of wings. A black-backed gull dived down at him from the sky, missed, swerved in flight, and rose to dive again. In a moment it was joined by others, six, seven, a dozen, black-backed and herring mixed. Nat dropped his hoe. The hoe was useless. Covering his head with his arms he ran towards the cottage. They kept coming at him
45 from the air, silent save for the beating wings. The terrible, fluttering wings. He could feel the blood on his hands, his wrists, his neck. Each stab of a swooping beak tore his flesh. If only he could keep them from his eyes.

1 *obliged:* thankful

8 *now* = now that

11 *bond (n):* link, strong connection

16 *make for sth.:* etwas anpeilen

18 *pace:* speed

19 *jerk:* ruckartige Bewegung

22 *poison sth.:* etwas vergiften

26 *else:* otherwise

28 *pickle sth.:* etwas pökeln

29 *let off a few barrels:* ein paar Ladungen abfeuern

29 *brute:* Vieh, Tier

34 *garn (sl):* nonsense

34 *windy (sl):* crazy

45 *save for:* except for

46 *wrist:* Handgelenk

46 *stab (n):* Stich

47 *swoop:* drop down to attack

Nothing else mattered. He must keep them from his eyes. They had not learnt yet how to cling to a shoulder, how to rip clothing, how to dive in mass upon the head, upon the body. But with each dive, with each attack, they became bolder. And they had no thought for themselves. When they dived
5 low and missed, they crashed, bruised and broken, on the ground. As Nat ran he stumbled, kicking their spent bodies in front of him.

He found the door, he hammered upon it with his bleeding hands. Because of the boarded windows no light shone. Everything was dark.

'Let me in,' he shouted, 'it's Nat. Let me in.'

10 He shouted loud to make himself heard above the whirr of the gulls' wings.

Then he saw the gannet, poised for the dive, above him in the sky. The gulls circled, retired, soared, one with another, against the wind. Only the gannet remained. One single gannet, above him in the sky. The wings folded
15 suddenly to its body. It dropped like a stone. Nat screamed and the door opened. He stumbled across the threshold, and his wife threw her weight against the door.

They heard the thud of the gannet as it fell.

His wife dressed his wounds. They were not deep. The backs of his hands
20 had suffered most, and his wrists. Had he not worn a cap they would have reached his head. As to the gannet ... the gannet could have split his skull.

The children were crying, of course. They had seen the blood on their father's hands.

'It's all right now,' he told them. 'I'm not hurt. Just a few scratches. You
25 play with Johnny, Jill. Mammy will wash these cuts.'

He half shut the door to the scullery, so that they could not see. His wife was ashen. She began running water from the sink.

'I saw them overhead,' she whispered. 'They began collecting just as Jill ran in with Mr Trigg. I shut the door fast, and it jammed. That's why I couldn't
30 open it at once, when you came.'

'Thank God they waited for me,' he said. 'Jill would have fallen at once. One bird alone would have done it.'

Furtively, so as not to alarm the children, they whispered together, as she bandaged his hands and the back of his neck.

35 'They're flying inland,' he said, 'thousands of them. Rooks, crows, all the bigger birds. I saw them from the bus-stop. They're making for the towns.'

'But what can they do, Nat?'

'They'll attack. Go for everyone out in the streets. Then they'll try the windows, the chimneys.'

40 'Why don't the authorities do something? Why don't they get the army, get machine-guns, anything?'

'There's been no time. Nobody's prepared. We'll hear what they have to say on the six o'clock news.'

Nat went back into the kitchen, followed by his wife. Johnny was playing
45 quietly on the floor. Only Jill looked anxious.

'I can hear the birds,' she said. 'Listen, Dad.'

2 *cling to sth.:* hold on to sth.
2 *rip sth.:* etwas zerreißen
4 *bold:* fearless
5 *bruised* [bru:zd]: injured
6 *spent:* verbraucht
12 *gannet:* Basstölpel
12 *be poised for sth.:* be ready for sth.
13 *retire:* sich zurückziehen
16 *threshold:* Türschwelle
19 *dress a wound* [wu:nd]: eine Wunde versorgen
21 *skull:* Schädel
27 *ashen (adj):* pale, white as ash
29 *jam:* klemmen
33 *furtive:* heimlich, verstohlen
40 *authorities:* Behörden

Nat listened. Muffled sounds came from the windows, from the door. Wings brushing the surface, sliding, scraping, seeking a way of entry. The sound of many bodies, pressed together, shuffling on the sills. Now and again came a thud, a crash, as some bird dived and fell. 'Some of them will
5   kill themselves that way,' he thought, 'but not enough. Never enough.'

'All right,' he said aloud, 'I've got boards over the windows, Jill. The birds can't get in.'

He went and examined all the windows. His work had been thorough. Every gap was closed. He would make extra certain, however. He found
10 wedges, pieces of old tin, strips of wood and metal, and fastened them at the sides to reinforce the boards. His hammering helped to deafen the sound of the birds, the shuffling, the tapping, and more ominous — he did not want his wife or the children to hear it — the splinter of cracked glass.

'Turn on the wireless,' he said, 'let's have the wireless.'
15 This would drown the sound also. He went upstairs to the bedrooms and reinforced the windows there. Now he could hear the birds on the roof, the scraping of claws, a sliding, jostling sound.

He decided they must sleep in the kitchen, keep up the fire, bring down the mattresses and lay them out on the floor. He was afraid of the bedroom
20 chimneys. The boards he had placed at the chimney bases might give way. In the kitchen they would be safe, because of the fire. He would have to make a joke of it. Pretend to the children they were playing at camp. If the worst happened, and the birds forced an entry down the bedroom chimneys, it would be hours, days perhaps, before they could break down the
25 doors. The birds would be imprisoned in the bedrooms. They could do no harm there. Crowded together, they would stifle and die.

He began to bring the mattresses downstairs. At sight of them his wife's eyes widened in apprehension. She thought the birds had already broken in upstairs.
30 'All right,' he said cheerfully, 'we'll all sleep together in the kitchen tonight. More cosy here by the fire. Then we shan't be worried by those silly old birds tapping at the windows.'

He made the children help him rearrange the furniture, and he took the precaution of moving the dresser, with his wife's help, across the window. It
35 fitted well. It was an added safeguard. The mattresses could now be lain, one beside the other, against the wall where the dresser had stood.

'We're safe enough now,' he thought, 'we're snug and tight, like an air-raid shelter. We can hold out. It's just the food that worries me. Food, and coal for the fire. We've enough for two or three days, not more. By that time ...'
40 No use thinking ahead as far as that. And they'd be giving directions on the wireless. People would be told what to do. And now, in the midst of many problems, he realized that it was dance music only coming over the air. Not Children's Hour, as it should have been. He glanced at the dial. Yes, they were on the Home Service all right. Dance records. He switched to the
45 Light programme. He knew the reason. The usual programmes had been abandoned. This only happened at exceptional times. Elections, and such. He tried to remember if it had happened in the war, during the heavy raids

1 *muffled:* gedämpft
3 *shuffle:* move restlessly
8 *thorough* ['θʌrə]: gründlich
10 *wedge:* Keil
11 *reinforce sth.* [ˌriːɪn'fɔːs]: etwas verstärken
11 *deafen sth.* ['defn]: etwas übertönen
12 *ominous:* threatening
15 *drown sth.:* etwas übertönen
17 *jostle:* move back and forth
26 *stifle:* die of lack of air
37 *snug:* warm and safe
42 *over the air:* from the radio
43 *dial:* Regler für die Senderwahl
47 *raid (n):* attack

on London. But of course. The BBC was not stationed in London during the war. The programmes were broadcast from other, temporary quarters. 'We're better off here,' he thought, 'we're better off here in the kitchen, with the windows and the doors boarded, than they are up in the towns. Thank
5 God we're not in the towns.'

At six o'clock the records ceased. The time signal was given. No matter if it scared the children, he must hear the news. There was a pause after the pips. Then the announcer spoke. His voice was solemn, grave. Quite different from midday.
10 'This is London,' he said. 'A National Emergency was proclaimed at four o'clock this afternoon. Measures are being taken to safeguard the lives and property of the population, but it must be understood that these are not easy to effect immediately, owing to the unforeseen and unparalleled nature of the present crisis. Every householder must take precautions to his own
15 building, and where several people live together, as in flats and apartments, they must unite to do the utmost they can to prevent entry. It is absolutely imperative that every individual stays indoors tonight, and that no one at all remains on the streets, or roads, or anywhere without doors. The birds, in vast numbers, are attacking anyone on sight, and have already begun an
20 assault upon buildings; but these, with due care, should be impenetrable. The population is asked to remain calm, and not to panic. Owing to the exceptional nature of the emergency, there will be no further transmission from any broadcasting station until seven a.m. tomorrow.'

They played the National Anthem. Nothing more happened. Nat switched
25 off the set. He looked at his wife. She stared back at him.

'What's it mean?' said Jill. 'What did the news say?'

'There won't be any more programmes tonight,' said Nat. 'There's been a breakdown at the BBC.'

'Is it the birds?' asked Jill. 'Have the birds done it?'
30 'No,' said Nat, 'it's just that everyone's very busy, and then of course they have to get rid of the birds, messing everything up, in the towns. Well, we can manage without the wireless for one evening.'

'I wish we had a gramophone,' said Jill, 'that would be better than nothing.'

She had her face turned to the dresser, backed against the windows. Try
35 as they did to ignore it, they were all aware of the shuffling, the stabbing, the persistent beating and sweeping of wings.

'We'll have supper early,' suggested Nat, 'something for a treat. Ask Mammy. Toasted cheese, eh? Something we all like?'

He winked and nodded at his wife. He wanted the look of dread, of appre-
40 hension, to go from Jill's face.

He helped with the supper, whistling, singing, making as much clatter as he could, and it seemed to him that the shuffling and the tapping were not so intense as they had been at first. Presently he went up to the bedrooms and listened, and he no longer heard the jostling for place upon the roof.
45 'They've got reasoning powers,' he thought, 'they know it's hard to break in here. They'll try elsewhere. They won't waste their time with us.'

8 *pip:* ‚beep'
8 *solemn, grave:* ernst
13 *effect sth.:* etwas realisieren
13 *owing to:* because of
20 *due (adj):* angemessen
20 *impenetrable:* unable to be entered
25 *set:* radio
31 *get rid of sth.:* etwas beseitigen
31 *mess everything up (infml):* cause chaos and confusion
36 *persistent:* never stopping
37 *treat (n):* Leckerbissen
39 *wink (v):* zwinkern
39 *nod (v):* nicken
39 *dread (n):* fear
41 *clatter:* Geklapper
45 *reasoning powers:* ability to think

Supper passed without incident, and then, when they were clearing away, they heard a new sound, droning, familiar, a sound they all knew and understood.

His wife looked up at him, her face alight. 'Its planes,' she said, 'they're
5 sending out planes after the birds. That's what I said they ought to do, all along. That will get them. Isn't that gun-fire? Can't you hear guns?'

It might be gun-fire, out at sea. Nat could not tell. Big naval guns might have an effect upon the gulls out at sea, but the gulls were inland now. The guns couldn't shell the shore, because of the population.

10 'It's good, isn't it,' said his wife, 'to hear the planes?'

And Jill, catching her enthusiasm, jumped up and down with Johnny. 'The planes will get the birds. The planes will shoot them.' Just then they heard a crash about two miles distant, followed by a second, then a third. The droning became more distant, passed away out to sea.

15 'What was that?' asked his wife. 'Were they dropping bombs on the birds?'

'I don't know,' answered Nat, 'I don't think so.'

He did not want to tell her that the sound they had heard was the crashing of aircraft. It was, he had no doubt, a venture on the part of the
20 authorities to send out reconnaissance forces, but they might have known the venture was suicidal. What could aircraft do against birds that flung themselves to death against propeller and fuselage, but hurtle to the ground themselves? This was being tried now, he supposed, over the whole country. And at a cost. Someone high up had lost his head.

25 'Where have the planes gone, Dad?' asked Jill.

'Back to base,' he said. 'Come on, now, time to tuck down for bed.'

It kept his wife occupied, undressing the children before the fire, seeing to the bedding, one thing and another, while he went round the cottage again, making sure that nothing had worked loose. There was no further
30 drone of aircraft, and the naval guns had ceased. 'Waste of life and effort,' Nat said to himself. 'We can't destroy enough of them that way. Cost too heavy. There's always gas. Maybe they'll try spraying with gas, mustard gas. We'll be warned first, of course, if they do. There's one thing, the best brains of the country will be on to it tonight.'

35 Somehow the thought reassured him. He had a picture of scientists, naturalists, technicians, and all those chaps they called the back-room boys, summoned to a council; they'd be working on the problem now. This was not a job for the government, for the chiefs-of-staff — they would merely carry out the orders of the scientists.

40 'They'll have to be ruthless,' he thought. 'Where the trouble's worst they'll have to risk more lives, if they use gas. All the livestock, too, and the soil — all contaminated. As long as everyone doesn't panic. That's the trouble. People panicking, losing their heads. The BBC was right to warn us of that.'

Upstairs in the bedrooms all was quiet. No further scraping and stabbing
45 at the windows. A lull in battle. Forces regrouping. Wasn't that what they called it, in the old war-time bulletins? The wind hadn't dropped, though. He could still hear it, roaring in the chimneys. And the sea breaking down on

2 *drone (v)*: make a low constant noise

4 *alight*: smiling

5 *all along*: the whole time

9 *shell sth.*: etwas mit Artillerie beschießen

19 *aircraft*: plane

19 *venture*: Versuch

20 *reconnaisance* [rɪ'kɒnɪsns] forces: Erkundungskräfte

22 *fuselage* ['fjuːzəlɑːʒ]: body of an aircraft

22 *hurtle*: fall

32 *mustard gas*: Senfgas

36 *chap (BE, infml)*: Typ

37 *summon sb. to sth. (fml)*: jdn. zu etwas zusammenrufen

38 *chief-of-staff*: oberster Befehlshaber der Streitkräfte

40 *ruthless*: rücksichtslos

41 *livestock*: farm animals

45 *lull (n)*: calm period

45 *regroup*: neu formieren

the shore. Then he remembered the tide. The tide would be on the turn.
Maybe the lull in battle was because of the tide. There was some law the
birds obeyed, and it was all to do with the east wind and the tide.

He glanced at his watch. Nearly eight o'clock. It must have gone high
5 water an hour ago. That explained the lull: the birds attacked with the flood
tide. It might not work that way inland, up country, but it seemed as if it was
so this way on the coast. He reckoned the time limit in his head. They had six
hours to go, without attack. When the tide turned again, around one-twenty
in the morning, the birds would come back ...

10 There were two things he could do. The first to rest, with his wife and the
children, and all of them snatch what sleep they could, until the small hours.
The second to go out, see how they were faring at the farm, see if the telephone was still working there, so that they might get news from the
exchange.

15 He called softly to his wife, who had just settled the children. She came
half-way up the stairs and he whispered to her.

'You're not to go,' she said at once, 'you're not to go and leave me alone
with the children. I can't stand it.'

Her voice rose hysterically. He hushed her, calmed her.

20 'All right,' he said, 'all right. I'll wait till morning. And we'll get the wireless
bulletin then too, at seven. But in the morning, when the tide ebbs again, I'll
try for the farm, and they may let us have bread and potatoes, and milk too.'

His mind was busy again, planning against emergency. They would not
have milked, of course, this evening. The cows would be standing by the
25 gate, waiting in the yard, with the household inside, battened behind boards,
as they were here at the cottage.

That is, if they had time to take precautions. He thought of the farmer,
Trigg, smiling at him from the car. There would have been no shooting party,
not tonight.

30 The children were asleep. His wife, still clothed, was sitting on her
mattress. She watched him, her eyes nervous.

'What are you going to do?' she whispered.

He shook his head for silence. Softly, stealthily, he opened the back door
and looked outside.

35 It was pitch dark. The wind was blowing harder than ever, coming in
steady gusts, icy, from the sea. He kicked at the step outside the door. It was
heaped with birds. There were dead birds everywhere. Under the windows,
against the walls. These were the suicides, the divers, the ones with broken
necks. Wherever he looked he saw dead birds. No trace of the living. The
40 living had flown seaward with the turn of the tide. The gulls would be riding
the seas now, as they had done in the forenoon.

In the far distance, on the hill where the tractor had been two days
before, something was burning. One of the aircraft that had crashed; the fire,
fanned by the wind, had set light to a stack.

45 He looked at the bodies of the birds, and he had a notion that if he heaped
them, one upon the other, on the window sills they would make added
protection for the next attack. Not much, perhaps, but something. The

7 *reckon sth.:* etwas
ausrechnen

11 *snatch sth.:* grab sth.

11 *small hours:* early hours

12 *fare:* get by

15 *settle sb.:* bring sb. to bed

19 *hush sb.:* get sb. to be quiet

25 *battened:* verrammelt

33 *stealthy:* very careful and
quiet

36 *gust:* sudden burst of wind

37 *heaped with:* übersät mit

41 *forenoon:* morning

44 *fan sth.:* etwas anfachen

44 *stack:* Heuhaufen

45 *notion:* idea

bodies would have to be clawed at, pecked, and dragged aside, before the living birds gained purchase on the sills and attacked the panes. He set to work in the darkness. It was queer; he hated touching them. The bodies were still warm and bloody. The blood matted their feathers. He felt his
5   stomach turn, but he went on with his work. He noticed, grimly, that every window-pane was shattered. Only the boards had kept the birds from breaking in. He stuffed the cracked panes with the bleeding bodies of the birds.

When he had finished he went back into the cottage. He barricaded the
10 kitchen door, made it doubly secure. He took off his bandages, sticky with the birds' blood, not with his own cuts, and put on fresh plaster.

His wife had made him cocoa and he drank it thirstily. He was very tired. 'All right,' he said, smiling, 'don't worry. We'll get through.'

He lay down on his mattress and closed his eyes. He slept at once. He
15 dreamt uneasily, because through his dreams there ran a thread of something forgotten. Some piece of work, neglected, that he should have done. Some precaution that he had known well but had not taken, and he could not put a name to it in his dreams. It was connected in some way with the burning aircraft and the stack upon the hill. He went on sleeping, though; he
20 did not awake. It was his wife shaking his shoulder that awoke him finally.

'They've begun,' she sobbed, 'they've started this last hour, I can't listen to it any longer, alone. There's something smelling bad too, something burning.'

Then he remembered. He had forgotten to make up the fire. It was smouldering, nearly out. He got up swiftly and lit the lamp. The hammering had
25 started at the windows and the doors, but it was not that he minded now. It was the smell of singed feathers. The smell filled the kitchen. He knew at once what it was. The birds were coming down the chimney, squeezing their way down to the kitchen range.

He got sticks and paper and put them on the embers, then reached for
30 the can of paraffin.

'Stand back,' he shouted to his wife, 'we've got to risk this.'

He threw the paraffin on to the fire. The flame roared up the pipe, and down upon the fire fell the scorched, blackened bodies of the birds.

The children woke, crying, 'What is it?' said Jill. 'What's happened?'
35 Nat had no time to answer. He was raking the bodies from the chimney, clawing them out on to the floor. The flames still roared, and the danger of the chimney catching fire was one he had to take. The flames would send away the living birds from the chimney top. The lower joint was the difficulty, though. This was choked with the smouldering helpless bodies of the
40 birds caught by fire. He scarcely heeded the attack on the windows and the door: let them beat their wings, break their beaks, lose their lives, in the attempt to force an entry into his home. They would not break in. He thanked God he had one of the old cottages, with small windows, stout walls. Not like the new council houses. Heaven help them up the lane, in the
45 new council houses.

'Stop crying,' he called to the children. 'There's nothing to be afraid of, stop crying.'

---

2 *gain purchase (fml):* find a place to land

4 *mat sth.:* verkleben

15 *thread:* Faden

16 *neglect sth.:* forget to do sth.

23 *smoulder:* schwelen, glimmen

25 *mind sth.:* pay attention to sth.

26 *singed* [sɪndʒd]: versengt

27 *squeeze one's way:* sich durchquetschen

28 *range:* Kochstelle

33 *scorched:* verkohlt

36 *claw (v):* harken, herauskratzen

38 *joint:* Anschluss

39 *choked:* verstopft

40 *heed sth.:* pay attention to sth.

43 *stout:* thick and strong

He went on raking at the burning, smouldering bodies as they fell into the fire.

'This'll fetch them,' he said to himself, 'the draught and the flames together. We're all right, as long as the chimney doesn't catch. I ought to be

5 shot for this. It's all my fault. Last thing I should have made up the fire. I knew there was something.' Amid the scratching and tearing at the window boards came the sudden homely striking of the kitchen clock. Three a.m. A little more than four hours yet to go. He could not be sure of the exact time of high water. He reckoned it would not turn much before half past seven,

10 twenty to eight.

'Light up the primus,' he said to his wife. 'Make us some tea, and the kids some cocoa. No use sitting around doing nothing.' That was the line. Keep her busy, and the children too. Move about, eat, drink; always best to be on the go.

15 He waited by the range. The flames were dying. But no more blackened bodies fell from the chimney. He thrust his poker up as far as it could go and found nothing. It was clear. The chimney was clear. He wiped the sweat from his forehead.

'Come on now, Jill,' he said, 'bring me some more sticks. We'll have a good

20 fire going directly.' She wouldn't come near him, though. She was staring at the heaped singed bodies of the birds.

'Never mind them,' he said, 'we'll put those in the passage when I've got the fire steady.'

The danger of the chimney was over. It could not happen again, not if the

25 fire was kept burning day and night.

'I'll have to get more fuel from the farm tomorrow,' he thought. 'This will never last. I'll manage, though. I can do all that with the ebb tide. It can be worked, fetching what we need, when the tide's turned. We've just got to adapt ourselves, that's all.' They drank tea and cocoa and ate slices of bread

30 and Bovril. Only half a loaf left, Nat noticed. Never mind though, they'd get by.

'Stop it,' said young Johnny, pointing to the windows with his spoon, 'stop it, you old birds.'

'That's right,' said Nat, smiling, 'we don't want the old beggars, do we?

35 Had enough of 'em.'

They began to cheer when they heard the thud of the suicide birds.

'There's another, Dad,' cried Jill, 'he's done for.'

'He's had it,' said Nat, 'there he goes, the blighter.'

This was the way to face up to it. This was the spirit. If they could keep

40 this up, hang on like this until seven, when the first news bulletin came through, they would not have done too badly.

'Give us a fag,' he said to his wife. 'A bit of a smoke will clear away the smell of the scorched feathers.'

'There's only two left in the packet,' she said. 'I was going to buy you some

45 from the Co-op.'

'I'll have one,' he said, 't'other will keep for a rainy day.'

3 *this'll fetch them:* das wird sie erledigen

7 *homely (BE):* cosy, familiar

11 *primus* = camping stove

12 *line:* course of action

16 *thrust sth.:* etwas stoßen

16 *poker:* Schürhaken

30 *Bovril*: thick, salty meat extract

34 *beggar (infml):* sb. you don't like

36 *cheer (v):* jubeln

37 *he's done for (infml):* den hat's erwischt

38 *he's had it:* den hat's erwischt

38 *blighter (BE, old-fashioned):* beggar

42 *fag (infml):* cigarette

46 *a rainy day:* a time when you need it

No sense trying to make the children rest. There was no rest to be got while the tapping and the scratching went on at the windows. He sat with one arm round his wife and the other round Jill, with Johnny on his mother's lap and the blankets heaped about them on the mattress.

5   'You can't help admiring the beggars,' he said, 'they've got persistence. You'd think they'd tire of the game, but not a bit of it.'

Admiration was hard to sustain. The tapping went on and on and a new rasping note struck Nat's ear, as though a sharper beak than any hitherto had come to take over from its fellows. He tried to remember the names of

10   birds, he tried to think which species would go for this particular job. It was not the tap of the woodpecker. That would be light and frequent. This was more serious, because if it continued long the wood would splinter as the glass had done. Then he remembered the hawks. Could the hawks have taken over from the gulls? Were there buzzards now upon the sills, using

15   talons as well as beaks? Hawks, buzzards, kestrels, falcons — he had forgotten the birds of prey. He had forgotten the gripping power of the birds of prey. Three hours to go, and while they waited the sound of the splintering wood, the talons tearing at the wood.

Nat looked about him, seeing what furniture he could destroy to fortify

20   the door. The windows were safe, because of the dresser. He was not certain of the door. He went upstairs, but when he reached the landing he paused and listened. There was a soft patter on the floor of the children's bedroom. The birds had broken through … He put his ear to the door. No mistake. He could hear the rustle of wings, and the light patter as they searched the floor.

25   The other bedroom was still clear. He went into it and began bringing out the furniture, to pile at the head of the stairs should the door of the children's bedroom go. It was a preparation. It might never be needed. He could not stack the furniture against the door, because it opened inward. The only possible thing was to have it at the top of the stairs.

30   'Come down, Nat, what are you doing?' called his wife.

'I won't be long,' he shouted. 'Just making everything shipshape up here.'

He did not want her to come; he did not want her to hear the pattering of the feet in the children's bedroom, the brushing of those wings against the door.

35   At five-thirty he suggested breakfast, bacon and fried bread, if only to stop the growing look of panic in his wife's eyes and to calm the fretful children. She did not know about the birds upstairs. The bedroom, luckily, was not over the kitchen. Had it been so she could not have failed to hear the sound of them, up there, tapping the boards. And the silly, senseless thud of

40   the suicide birds, the death-and-glory boys, who flew into the bedroom, smashing their heads against the walls. He knew them of old, the herring gulls. They had no brains. The black-backs were different, they knew what they were doing. So did the buzzards, the hawks …

He found himself watching the clock, gazing at the hands that went so

45   slowly round the dial. If his theory was not correct, if the attack did not cease with the turn of the tide, he knew they were beaten. They could not continue through the long day without air, without rest, without more fuel,

7 *sustain sth.:* keep sth. up

8 *rasping note:* kratzendes Geräusch

8 *hitherto* [ˌhɪðəˈtuː] *(fml):* until now

9 *fellow:* Genosse

11 *woodpecker:* Specht

13 *hawk:* Habicht

15 *talon:* Kralle

16 *bird of prey:* Raubvogel

19 *fortify sth.:* make sth. stronger

21 *landing (n):* Treppenabsatz

24 *patter:* soft noise

26 *pile sth.:* etwas stapeln

28 *stack sth.:* pile sth.

31 *shipshape (adj):* in order

40 *death-and-glory boy:* soldier who dies to become famous

41 *of old (fml):* from earlier times

45 *dial:* Zifferblatt

46 *cease:* end

without ... his mind raced. He knew there were so many things they needed to withstand siege. They were not fully prepared. They were not ready. It might be that it would be safer in the towns after all. If he could get a message through, on the farm telephone, to his cousin, only a short journey
5 by train up country they might be able to hire a car. That would be quicker — hire a car between tides ...

His wife's voice, calling his name, drove away the sudden, desperate desire for sleep.

'What is it? What now?' he said sharply.

10 'The wireless,' said his wife. 'I've been watching the clock. It's nearly seven.'

'Don't twist the knob,' he said, impatient for the first time, 'it's on the Home where it is. They'll speak from the Home.'

They waited. The kitchen clock struck seven. There was no sound. No
15 chimes, no music. They waited until a quarter past, switching to the Light. The result was the same. No news bulletin came through.

'We've heard wrong,' he said, 'they won't be broadcasting until eight o'clock.'

They left it switched on, and Nat thought of the battery, wondered how
20 much power was left in it. It was generally recharged when his wife went shopping in the town. If the battery failed they would not hear the instructions.

'It's getting light,' whispered his wife, 'I can't see it, but I can feel it. And the birds aren't hammering so loud.'

25 She was right. The rasping, tearing sound grew fainter every moment. So did the shuffling, the jostling for place upon the step, upon the sills. The tide was on the turn. By eight there was no sound at all. Only the wind. The children, lulled at last by the stillness, fell asleep. At half past eight Nat switched the wireless off.

30 'What are you doing? We'll miss the news,' said his wife.

'There isn't going to be any news,' said Nat. 'We've got to depend upon ourselves.'

He went to the door and slowly pulled away the barricades. He drew the bolts, and kicking the bodies from the step outside the door breathed the
35 cold air. He had six working hours before him, and he knew he must reserve his strength for the right things, not waste it in any way. Food, and light, and fuel; these were the necessary things. If he could get them in sufficiency, they could endure another night.

He stepped into the garden, and as he did so he saw the living birds. The
40 gulls had gone to ride the sea, as they had done before; they sought sea food, and the buoyancy of the tide, before they returned to the attack. Not so the land birds. They waited and watched. Nat saw them, on the hedgerows, on the soil, crowded in the trees, outside in the field, line upon line of birds, all still, doing nothing.

45 He went to the end of his small garden. The birds did not move. They went on watching him.

2 *withstand sth.:* survive sth.
12 *knob* [nɒb]: Regler, Knopf
13 *the Home:* name of a radio station
15 *chime:* sound of a bell ringing
25 *faint (adj):* weak
28 *lull sb.:* jdn. einlullen
33 *draw the bolts:* die Riegel zurückziehen
37 *in sufficiency* [səˈfɪʃnsi]: in ausreichender Menge
41 *buoyancy* [ˈbɔɪənsi]: Auftrieb

'I've got to get food,' said Nat to himself, 'I've got to go to the farm to find food.'

He went back to the cottage. He saw to the windows and the doors. He went upstairs and opened the children's bedroom. It was empty, except for
5 the dead birds on the floor. The living were out there, in the garden, in the fields. He went downstairs.

'I'm going to the farm,' he said.

His wife clung to him. She had seen the living birds from the open door.

'Take us with you,' she begged, 'we can't stay here alone. I'd rather die
10 than stay here alone.'

He considered the matter. He nodded.

'Come on, then,' he said, 'bring baskets, and Johnny's pram. We can load up the pram.'

They dressed against the biting wind, wore gloves and scarves. His wife
15 put Johnny in the pram. Nat took Jill's hand.

'The birds,' she whimpered, 'they're all out there, in the fields.'

'They won't hurt us,' he said, 'not in the light.'

They started walking across the field towards the stile, and the birds did not move. They waited, their heads turned to the wind.
20 When they reached the turning to the farm, Nat stopped and told his wife to wait in the shelter of the hedge with the two children.

'But I want to see Mrs Trigg,' she protested. 'There are lots of things we can borrow, if they went to market yesterday; not only bread, and ...'

'Wait here,' Nat interrupted. 'I'll be back in a moment.'
25 The cows were lowing, moving restlessly in the yard, and he could see a gap in the fence where the sheep had knocked their way through, to roam unchecked in the front garden before the farm-house. No smoke came from the chimneys. He was filled with misgivings. He did not want his wife or the children to go down to the farm.
30 'Don't jib now,' said Nat, harshly, 'do what I say.'

She withdrew with the pram into the hedge, screening herself and the children from the wind.

He went down alone to the farm. He pushed his way through the herd of bellowing cows, which turned this way and that, distressed, their udders
35 full. He saw the car standing by the gate, not put away in the garage. The windows of the farm-house were smashed. There were many dead gulls lying in the yard and around the house. The living birds perched on the group of trees behind the farm and on the roof of the house. They were quite still. They watched him.
40 Jim's body lay in the yard ... what was left of it. When the birds had finished, the cows had trampled him. His gun was beside him. The door of the house was shut and bolted, but as the windows were smashed it was easy to lift them and climb through. Trigg's body was close to the telephone. He must have been trying to get through to the exchange when the birds
45 came for him. The receiver was hanging loose, the instrument torn from the wall. No sign of Mrs Trigg. She would be upstairs. Was it any use going up?

12 *pram:* Kinderwagen

16 *whimper (v):* winseln

25 *low (v):* muhen

30 *jib (v) (infml):* protest

31 *screen sb. from sth:* jdn. vor etwas schützen

34 *bellow:* make a loud noise

34 *distressed:* verzweifelt

34 *udder:* Euter

37 *perch:* sit

Sickened, Nat knew what he would find. 'Thank God,' he said to himself, 'there were no children.'

He forced himself to climb the stairs, but half-way he turned and descended again. He could see her legs, protruding from the open bedroom
5 door. Beside her were the bodies of the black-backed gulls, and an umbrella, broken.

'It's no use,' thought Nat, 'doing anything. I've only got five hours, less than that. The Triggs would understand. I must load up with what I can find.'

He tramped back to his wife and children.
10 'I'm going to fill up the car with stuff,' he said. 'I'll put coal in it, and paraffin for the primus. We'll take it home and return for a fresh load.'

'What about the Triggs?' asked his wife.

'They must have gone to friends,' he said.

'Shall I come and help you, then?'
15 'No; there's a mess down there. Cows and sheep all over the place. Wait, I'll get the car. You can sit in it.'

Clumsily he backed the car out of the yard and into the lane. His wife and the children could not see Jim's body from there.

'Stay here,' he said, 'never mind the pram. The pram can be fetched later.
20 I'm going to load the car.'

Her eyes watched his all the time. He believed she understood, otherwise she would have suggested helping him to find the bread and groceries.

They made three journeys altogether, backwards and forwards between their cottage and the farm, before he was satisfied they had everything they
25 needed. It was surprising, once he started thinking, how many things were necessary. Almost the most important of all was planking for the windows. He had to go round searching for timber. He wanted to renew the boards on all the windows at the cottage. Candles, paraffin, nails, tinned stuff; the list was endless. Besides all that, he milked three of the cows. The rest, poor
30 brutes, would have to go on bellowing.

On the final journey he drove the car to the bus-stop, got out, and went to the telephone box. He waited a few minutes, jangling the receiver. No good, though. The line was dead. He climbed on to a bank and looked over the countryside, but there was no sign of life at all, nothing in the fields but
35 the waiting, watching birds. Some of them slept — he could see the beaks tucked into the feathers.

'You'd think they'd be feeding,' he said to himself, 'not just standing in that way.'

Then he remembered. They were gorged with food. They had eaten their
40 fill during the night. That was why they did not move this morning ... .

No smoke came from the chimneys of the council houses. He thought of the children who had run across the fields the night before.

'I should have known,' he thought, 'I ought to have taken them home with me.'
45 He lifted his face to the sky. It was colourless and grey. The bare trees on the landscape looked bent and blackened by the east wind. The cold did not affect the living birds, waiting out there in the fields.

4 *protrude:* herausragen
17 *clumsy:* ungeschickt
26 *planking (n):* boards
27 *timber:* wood
32 *jangle sth.:* hold sth. loosely
39 *gorged:* vollgestopft

'This is the time they ought to get them,' said Nat, 'they're a sitting target now. They must be doing this all over the country. Why don't our aircraft take off now and spray them with mustard gas? What are all our chaps doing? They must know, they must see for themselves.'

5 He went back to the car and got into the driver's seat.

'Go quickly past that second gate,' whispered his wife. 'The postman's lying there. I don't want Jill to see.'

He accelerated. The little Morris bumped and rattled along the lane. The children shrieked with laughter.

10 'Up-a-down, up-a-down,' shouted young Johnny.

It was a quarter to one by the time they reached the cottage. Only an hour to go.

'Better have cold dinner,' said Nat. 'Hot up something for yourself and the children, some of that soup. I've no time to eat now. I've got to unload all this 15 stuff.'

He got everything inside the cottage. It could be sorted later. Give them all something to do during the long hours ahead. First he must see to the windows and the doors.

He went round the cottage methodically, testing every window, every 20 door. He climbed on to the roof also, and fixed boards across every chimney, except the kitchen. The cold was so intense he could hardly bear it, but the job had to be done. Now and again he would look up, searching the sky for aircraft. None came. As he worked he cursed the inefficiency of the authorities.

25 'It's always the same,' he muttered, 'they always let us down. Muddle, muddle, from the start. No plan, no real organization. And we don't matter, down here. That's what it is. The people up country have priority. They're using gas up there, no doubt, and all the aircraft. We've got to wait and take what comes.'

30 He paused, his work on the bedroom chimney finished, and looked out to sea. Something was moving out there. Something grey and white amongst the breakers.

'Good old Navy,' he said, 'they never let us down. They're coming down channel, they're turning in the bay.'

35 He waited, straining his eyes, watering in the wind, towards the sea. He was wrong, though. It was not ships. The Navy was not there. The gulls were rising from the sea. The massed flocks in the fields, with ruffled feathers, rose in formation from the ground, and wing to wing soared upwards to the sky.

40 The tide had turned again.

Nat climbed down the ladder and went inside the kitchen. The family were at dinner. It was a little after two. He bolted the door, put up the barricade, and lit the lamp.

'It's night-time,' said young Johnny.

45 His wife had switched on the wireless once again, but no sound came from it.

1 *sitting target:* easy target to hit
8 *accelerate:* Gas geben
8 *Morris*°*:* name of a British car
9 *shriek:* cry out
23 *curse sb./sth.:* jdn./etwas verfluchen
23 *inefficiency:* inability to work effectively
26 *muddle:* chaos
33 *let sb. down:* disappoint sb.
35 *water (v):* tränen
37 *ruffled:* gespreizt

'I've been all round the dial,' she said, 'foreign stations, and that lot. I can't get anything.'

'Maybe they have the same trouble,' he said, 'maybe it's the same right through Europe.'

5 She poured out a plateful of the Triggs' soup, cut him a large slice of the Triggs' bread, and spread their dripping upon it.

They ate in silence. A piece of the dripping ran down young Johnny's chin and fell on to the table.

'Manners, Johnny,' said Jill, 'you should learn to wipe your mouth.'

10 The tapping began at the windows, at the door. The rustling, the jostling, the pushing for position on the sills. The first thud of the suicide gulls upon the step.

'Won't America do something?' said his wife. 'They've always been our allies, haven't they? Surely America will do something?'

15 Nat did not answer. The boards were strong against the windows, and on the chimneys too. The cottage was filled with stores, with fuel, with all they needed for the next few days. When he had finished dinner he would put the stuff away, stack it neatly, get everything shipshape, handy-like. His wife could help him, and the children too. They'd tire themselves out, between 20 now and a quarter to nine, when the tide would ebb; then he'd tuck them down on their mattresses, see that they slept good and sound until three in the morning.

He had a new scheme for the windows, which was to fix barbed wire in front of the boards. He had brought a great roll of it from the farm. The 25 nuisance was, he'd have to work at this in the dark, when the lull came between nine and three. Pity he had not thought of it before. Still, as long as the wife slept, and the kids, that was the main thing.

The smaller birds were at the window now. He recognized the light tap-tapping of their beaks, and the soft brush of their wings. The hawks ignored 30 the windows. They concentrated their attack upon the door. Nat listened to the tearing sound of splintering wood, and wondered how many million years of memory were stored in those little brains, behind the stabbing beaks, the piercing eyes, now giving them this instinct to destroy mankind with all the deft precision of machines.

35 'I'll smoke that last fag,' he said to his wife. 'Stupid of me, it was the one thing I forgot to bring back from the farm.'

He reached for it, switched on the silent wireless. He threw the empty packet on the fire, and watched it burn.

From: Daphne du Maurier, The Apple Tree, *1952*

1 *that lot:* similar things

6 *dripping (n):* fat and juices that come out of meat during cooking

9 *manners:* Manieren

14 *ally* ['ælaɪ]: Verbündeter

16 *store:* Vorrat

18 *handy-like (infml):* ready for use

21 *sound (adj):* fest, ungestört

23 *scheme (n)* [skiːm]: plan

23 *barbed wire:* Stacheldraht

25 *nuisance:* problem, disadvantage

33 *piercing (adj):* bohrend

33 *mankind:* die Menschheit

34 *deft:* skilled

INFOBOX	Daphne du Maurier

Daphne du Maurier was born in London in 1907. She came from a well-known family of actors, writers and artists. These connections helped her to reach early success with her first stories and novels. Bestsellers like Jamaica Inn (1936) and Rebecca (1938) made du Maurier famous and independently wealthy. She died in Cornwall in 1989, where she had spent most of her life.

1 a With the help of your while-reading notes (Nat's diary), outline the development of the 'bird threat' from an interesting observation to a life-and-death struggle.

   b Compare outlines with a partner. Add any missing information.

2 a ANALYSIS Form four groups. Each group examines the reaction of one character or group of characters to the emerging crisis:

   – Nat Hocken
   – Nat's wife and the children
   – Jim and Mr and Mrs Trigg
   – the outside world

   b Form new groups in which at least one person from each of the four groups is present. Discuss how different people react differently to the crisis.

   c Explain why you think the author chose someone like Nat Hocken to be the focal point of the narrative.

3 Describe the atmosphere in ll. 5–10 on p. 40.

4 a Choose one of the two excerpts and examine how du Maurier creates suspense.

      p. 45, l. 32 – p. 46, l. 9
      OR
      p. 46, l. 42 – p. 47, l. 34

   b Get together with a partner who has chosen the other excerpt and compare results.

   c Together with your partner, make a list of ways to create suspense in writing.

5 a The characters in the story offer various explanations for the birds' aggressive behaviour. Make a list of these examples and the characters who propose them.

   b Discuss in your class whether the author offers an explanation for the birds' sudden change of behaviour.

6 **WRITING** Choose a theme from the list below, or make up one of your own.
Use it to write an interpretation of the story (about 300 words).

- Nature strikes back
- Technology and superiority
- Human beings and their relationship to nature

7 **SPEAKING** If du Maurier's story took place in our time, would the outcome be any different?
Prepare and conduct a discussion.

a Divide the class into two groups. One group collects arguments why the outcome
would be the same, the other group concentrates on arguments why t would be different.
Use information from the story and your own ideas.

b Decide on the form of the discussion, e.g. debate, fish bowl, and plan it accordingly.

c In your group, prepare an opening statement.

d Hold the discussion. Make sure to use appropriate discussion vocabulary.

8 Alfred Hitchcock bought the film rights to du Maurier's story. His film *The Birds* was released in 1963.
Watch the film and report to your class which aspects of the story Hitchcock retained and
which he changed.

ACKNOWLEDGEMENTS

Titelbild
Fotolia/kefca

Bildquellen
Shutterstock (S. 5: Dimec; S. 26: Nazhna; S. 28: panki; S. 34: okili77;
S. 36: Yurchenko Yulia)

Textquellen
S. 5–21 Arthur Conan Doyle: "A scandal in Bohemia" In: *The Strand Maga-zine*, July 1891;
S. 23–24 Heiko Postma: "John Watson, M. D. von Arthur Conan Doyle"
In: *Galerie der Detektive. 123 Portraits von Sherlock Holmes bis Nero Wolfe*.
Postma, Heiko und Rainer Wagner (Hrsg.). Hannover: Revonnah Verlag,
1997;
S. 26 Alyssa Rosenberg: "Sherlock Holmes Meets the 21st Century"
The Atlantic Monthly Group, 19.10.2010 http://www.theatlantic.com/
entertainment/archive/2010/10/sherlock-holmes-meets-the-21st-century/
64788/ (Stand: 07.04.2016);
S. 28–31 Edgar Allan Poe: "The tell-tale heart" In: *The Pioneer*, January 1843;
S. 33 Hans-Dieter Gelfert: "Geistige Gänsehaut" In: *Der Spiegel* 4/2009.
http://www.spiegel.de/spiegel/print/d-63637480.html (Stand: 07.04.2016);
S. 36–61 Daphne du Maurier: "The Birds" In: *The Apple Tree*. London: Victor
Gollancz Ltd. © the estate of Daphne du Maurier 1952.